Social Issues
in Literature

Justice in Arthur Miller's
The Crucible

Other Books in the Social Issues in Literature Series:

Social Issues in Literature

Justice in Arthur Miller's *The Crucible*

Claudia Durst Johnson, Book Editor

GREENHAVEN PRESS
A part of Gale, Cengage Learning

Detroit • New York • San Francisco • New Haven, Conn • Waterville, Maine • London

Christine Nasso, *Publisher*
Elizabeth Des Chenes, *Managing Editor*

© 2009 Greenhaven Press, a part of Gale, Cengage Learning

Gale and Greenhaven Press are registered trademarks used herein under license.

For more information, contact:
Greenhaven Press
27500 Drake Rd.
Farmington Hills, MI 48331-3535
Or you can visit our Internet site at gale.cengage.com

For product information and technology assistance, contact us at

Gale Customer Support, 1-800-877-4253
For permission to use material from this text or product, submit all requests online at www.cengage.com/permissions

Further permissions questions can be emailed to permissionrequest@cengage.com

Articles in Greenhaven Press anthologies are often edited for length to meet page requirements. In addition, original titles of these works are changed to clearly present the main thesis and to explicitly indicate the author's opinion. Every effort is made to ensure that Greenhaven Press accurately reflects the original intent of the authors. Every effort has been made to trace the owners of copyrighted material.

Cover photograph © Hulton-Deutsch Collection/Corbis.

LIBRARY OF CONGRESS CATALOGING-IN-PUBLICATION DATA

Justice in Arthur Miller's The crucible / Claudia Durst Johnson, book editor.
   p. cm. -- (Social issues in literature)
   Includes bibliographical references and index.
   ISBN 978-0-7377-4390-6
   ISBN 978-0-7377-4389-0 (pbk.)
   1. Miller, Arthur, 1915-2005. 2. Crucible. 3. Justice in literature. I. Johnson, Claudia D.
   PS3525.I5156C7347 2009
   812'.52--dc22

                                                                    2008051754

Printed in the United States of America
1 2 3 4 5 6 7 13 12 11 10 09

Contents

Chapter 3: Contemporary Perspectives on Legal Issues

Introduction

In 1692 in the village of Salem in the Massachusetts Bay Colony, a series of horrific events occurred that has served as a symbol of mass injustice and added the term "witch-hunting" to our vocabulary. Within a period of twelve months, twenty people were executed in Salem, and hundreds, including babies and young children, were jailed. Many died in the overcrowded jail. Hundreds more lost everything they owned as well as their good standing in the community by falsely confessing to witchcraft to avoid execution.

The Salem witch hunts, which Arthur Miller dramatized 258 years later in his play, *The Crucible*, reflect an abundance of motives, ironies, hysteria, and chaos common to cases of injustice throughout the history of the United States. The witch trials were held because of fanatical religion, hatred, vengeance, fear, and greed. Much can be explained by the religious beliefs of the Puritans and their reactions to grave circumstances in the years preceding the trials. New England had suffered disaster after disaster in the decades before the trials, including fires that devastated towns and villages, Indian raids, and plagues that wiped out a large portion of the population. The Puritans' theology led them to believe that these were punishments of an angry God, displeased by their toleration of the devil and his witches in their midst. When the idea of witchcraft arose, the authorities welcomed it and overreacted in their madness. Similar disasters set off mass hysteria in the twentieth century, such as Russian expansion after World War II, the fear of socialism's deleterious effect on capitalism, and the terrorist attacks of September 11, 2001. Each has led to fear, hysteria, rash judgments, and injustice, as disaster did in Salem.

Other motives played into the witch hunts and accusations in Miller's play: hatred of those (like John Proctor and Giles

Corey) who challenged authorities, vengeance against enemies and rivals (like Rebecca Nurse and Elizabeth Proctor), a need for self-protection (Reverend Parris's motive), sexual passion and jealousy (on the part of Abigail Williams), lust for land (Thomas Putnam's object), and the whole community's fear of the courts.

In the end, justice was perverted. People around Salem were arrested, tried, and sentenced to death simply on the accusations of witchcraft made or engineered by their enemies. No hard evidence held any weight. Instead the courts accepted "spectral evidence." For example, a girl, like Abigail Williams, could accuse an old woman, like Rebecca Nurse, of choking her in her bed at a specific time on a specific day. Eyewitnesses could, and did, bravely come forward to testify that such an accusation could not be true because they had seen the accused in church at that time. But the court ignored the hard evidence of eyewitnesses, claiming that, although the accused woman's body may have been in church, her wicked spirit had flown through the air and was choking the victim at the same time. If the accused confessed, her life would be saved, but she would be an outcast forever and all her property would be confiscated. Some confessions were obtained through torture. In *The Crucible* old Giles Corey is slowly pressed to death with stones as he refuses to confess.

The injustice of the Salem witch trials was similarily repeated in the 1940s and 1950s when radicals were hunted down (like the so-called Salem witches) and accused of planning to overthrow the U.S. government. Thousands of people were investigated and spied on. These "witch-hunts" were well underway when Miller wrote *The Crucible*. At the time, it was no secret that the play was not only about Salem, but also about the cold war.

The fear and rash judgments of the Salem witch trials were resurrected most recently following the 9/11 attacks in

2001. Individual rights and democracy itself have been sacrificed in the course of fighting terrorism.

The similarities in the injustices perpetrated in *The Crucible*, during the cold war, and in our post-9/11 society are explored in the articles that follow in this book. Chapter one is composed of biographical selections. The articles in chapter two include Miller's own analysis of *The Crucible*; the various ways in which Salem's religious superstition replaces conscience, rational law, and justice; the loss of justice in the mass hysteria encouraged by Salem's authorities; and the challenge to the authorities by several Salem citizens. Chapter three takes a look at relevant contemporary issues of justice, including the U.S. Supreme Court ruling granting legal rights to Arab prisoners arrested during the invasions of Afghanistan and Iraq and the use of DNA to free wrongly convicted people.

Chronology

1915

Arthur Miller is born on October 17 in New York City.

1929

Miller's father's business suffers during the Great Depression, and the family moves to Brooklyn, New York.

1934

Miller attends the University of Michigan, where he begins to write plays.

1939

Miller writes scripts for the Federal Theatre Project and then radio plays for CBS and NBC.

1944

The Man Who Had All the Luck, Miller's first Broadway play, opens but lasts for only four performances.

1945

Miller publishes his first novel, *Focus*.

1947

Miller's second play, *All My Sons*, opens on Broadway. It wins two Tony Awards. Miller becomes involved in anti-Fascist, left-wing activities.

1949

Miller's play *Death of a Salesman* opens on Broadway. It wins the Pulitzer Prize for Drama and six Tony Awards.

1950

Miller adapts Henrik Ibsen's *An Enemy of the People* for the stage.

1953

The Crucible opens on Broadway.

1954

Miller is denied a passport by the State Department because of his leftist associations. Many believe the denial is in retaliation for *The Crucible*.

1955

Miller's one-act plays, *A View from the Bridge* and *A Memory of Two Mondays*, open in New York.

1956

Miller is called to testify before the House Un-American Activities Committee. He refuses to provide the names of people suspected to be communists and communist sympathizers. Miller divorces his first wife, Mary Slattery, and marries actress Marilyn Monroe.

1957

Miller is convicted for contempt of Congress.

1958

A court of appeals reverses Miller's conviction for contempt of Congress.

1961

Miller and Marilyn Monroe divorce. He marries photographer Ingeborg Morath.

1964

Miller's plays, *After the Fall* and *Incident at Vichy*, open in New York.

1968

Miller's play, *The Price*, opens on Broadway.

1972

The Crucible has a revival in New York.

1986

The Crucible has another revival in New York and Washington, D.C.

1987

Miller publishes his autobiography, *Timebends*.

1989

The Crucible has a revival in New Haven.

1990

The Crucible has a revival in New York and London.

1996

A film version of *The Crucible* is released.

2005

Arthur Miller dies in February.

Background on Arthur Miller

Preparation for *The Crucible*

Jeffrey Helterman

Jeffrey Helterman is a widely published scholar and a specialist in the works of Arthur Miller and Bernard Malamud. He is the author of American Novelists Since WWII.

One of Arthur Miller's earliest projects, a journal compiled of interviews with veterans of World War II, arose from his interest in the causes of the war, that is, the fight against fascism, which had similarities with the Puritan theocracy of The Crucible. *In* An Enemy of the People, *Miller's adaptation of Norwegian playwright Henrik Ibsen's play, the main character, who interferes with his town's plans to build a spa, is a hero in the mold of John Proctor.* The Crucible *targets misuse of power, mass paranoia, false allegations, and the corruption of the courts charged with upholding justice. The play got a cool reception at its opening in the United States, where similar political issues were being played out. Two years later, in 1955, Miller found himself in John Proctor's position and was found guilty of contempt of Congress.*

Arthur Miller was born in Manhattan, the son of a middle-class ladies' coat manufacturer and a schoolteacher mother. . . . Although he went to grammar school in then fashionable Harlem, Miller was forced to move to Brooklyn when his father suffered major losses right before the Depression. . . .

Early Sense of Social Justice

In 1944, Miller toured army camps as a researcher, gathering background material for the filming of Ernie Pyle's *Story of GI Joe* (1945). Miller turned his research into a wartime journal

Jeffrey Helterman, "Arthur Miller," *Twentieth-Century American Dramatists*, Detroit, MI: Gale Research Company, 1981. Copyright © 1981 Gale Research Company. Reproduced by permission of Gale, a part of Cengage Learning.

called *Situation Normal,* which was published that year. He worked hard to keep his journal free of the flag-waving patriotism that was the stuff of most Hollywood treatments of the war effort. As he toured such places as Fort Dix, Camp Croft, and Fort Benning, he became increasingly concerned with the soldiers' thinking about the aims of the war. His description of a GI back from New Georgia in the southwest Pacific is a striking revelation of the new perceptions brought to the average American soldier by life in combat. . . .

Early Influence of Social Playwright Ibsen

Miller's first successful play, *All My Sons,* bears the stamp of [Henrik] Ibsen's influence in its style, its theme, and even its plot. . . .

The thematic concerns of *All My Sons* are also Ibsen's. Like Gregers Werle in *The Wild Duck,* Chris Keller is an idealist who insists on dredging up the past so that the truth may set everyone free. As in Ibsen's play, the revelation of the truth destroys everyone it is supposed to cleanse. The secret hidden in the past is basically the same as that which plagues Gregers's father in *The Wild Duck.* Chris's father, Joe Keller, has sent the air force the defective engine parts which caused the deaths of twenty-one flyers; then he left his partner to take the blame. The father's guilt is magnified because his eldest son, Larry, is a pilot who is missing and presumed dead. Although Larry did not fly one of the defective P-40s, his death becomes central to the moral crisis of the story. . . .

Social Issues in Early Plays

When *All My Sons* won the New York Drama Critics Circle Award in 1947, Miller was established as an important young playwright, particularly since the competition included Eugene O'Neill's *The Iceman Cometh.* In retrospect, the critics' choice seems somewhat off the mark; Miller's work is a solid piece and an important milestone in his career, but it is not a match for O'Neill's masterpiece.

The critics may just have been foresighted. Miller's next play, which won their award in 1949, was comparable to O'Neill at his best. *Death of a Salesman* was that wonder of wonders, a masterpiece that came easily. The play tells how its protagonist, Willy Loman, a middle-class salesman whose youth is but a memory, decides to end his life. He is loved by his wife, Linda, and he has two sons, Biff and Happy, whom he has tried to raise to become men of influence and power. Biff, the older son, now in his thirties, has not lived up to Willy's expectations, goals which were set when Biff was a high-school football hero. When Biff's plans to borrow money to go into a sporting goods business fail, he confronts Willy with his version of the truth and then breaks down and weeps. Willy feels at last that his son loves him and commits suicide in the automobile so that Biff can have the life insurance money. . . .

The critical and financial triumph of *Death of a Salesman* catapulted Miller into the front rank of American dramatists. The play won Miller's second Drama Critics Circle Award and a Pulitzer Prize in 1949. The royalties for *All My Sons* had paid for Miller's house in Brooklyn, but with Miller's characteristic disdain for props, it had remained half-furnished. The more than two-year run of *Death of a Salesman* furnished the house handsomely. In addition to the royalties for the Broadway production, there were two road companies that performed the play, soon to become a movie, and, perhaps most lucrative of all, a part of the repertory of almost every local theatre in the country.

In 1950, Miller's adaptation of Ibsen's *An Enemy of the People* was produced on Broadway. The work strengthened Miller's already strong ties to Ibsen, but it also signaled his interest in a new type of hero. Up to this point Miller's heroes dissipated their energies in the pursuit of misguided ideals. For the most part, Ibsen's heroes are of this mold as well, but Peter Stockmann's courage in the face of his town's moral cowardice needs no defensive explanation like that which Charley gives for Willy Loman at Willy's funeral. Stockmann is a doctor who refuses to permit the town to build a spa after he finds disease in the water supply. He becomes the town's enemy because his rectitude threatens its profits. The chief action of the play is the gradual turning of the entire town against a man who was once one of its most respected citizens.

A hero of this kind emerges in Miller's next play, *The Crucible* (1953). . . .

Justice in Salem and Washington, D.C.

The Crucible is set during the Salem witchcraft trials and the analogies with Senator Joseph McCarthy's "witch-hunts" for communists were immediately perceived by the critics. Miller's comments on the play at this time encouraged such comparisons and the play's relevance becomes even more striking a few years later because Miller himself was called (in 1956) before the House Committee on Un-American Activities. In a classic case of life imitating art, Miller took the precise position Proctor took before his Puritan judges. Just as Proctor is willing to implicate himself but refuses to name other dabblers with witchcraft, so Miller named himself, but refused to identify any others involved in communist-front activities. . . .

Since his concern is with the sources of the madness which was plaguing his own time as well as that of the Puritans, Miller explores the multi-faceted causes for the growth of the witch-hunt. The first sources, social or economic, are rational. Rev. Parris, the village minister, finds it useful to explain his daughter's indecent behavior by attributing it to witchcraft rather than to his own inability to raise her properly, and Mr. Putnam, the town's richest man, finds great advantage in having his rival landowners charged with witchcraft. Because of her testimony, Abigail Williams, a serving girl and something of a slut, raises herself to a position of power in the town. As

Actors Winona Ryder (left) and Daniel Day-Lewis in the film The Crucible, *produced by playwright Arthur Miller in 1996.* The Kobal Collection. Reproduced by permission.

the fever grows, however, its sources lie more and more in the irrationality of the human psyche as both individual and mass hysteria take over the town. Paranoia surfaces: Mrs. Putnam's unfocused despair over the loss of her infants in childbirth turns to a more comforting hatred of Rebecca Nurse. Both Mrs. Putnam and Rev. Parris see a kind of inverse election in being tormented by the devil. Miller very convincingly describes the "positive" effects of paranoia. The "victims" of the witches begin to value themselves more highly than those who have been left alone, since it comforts them to know that someone, even Satan, is constantly watching out for them. The culmination of the mass hysteria occurs when the girls of Salem, egged on by the calculated deceptions of Abigail truly believe, that they see the devil in the form of a gigantic bird.

False Accusation

Miller also observes the tremendous force that mere accusation had at this time, something that was evident as well in the McCarthy witch-hunts. A man's career could be ruined if he were merely asked, "Are you now or have you ever been a member of the Communist party?" The power of accusation is seen in the town's reaction to the charges made by two servants, Abigail, who deliberately uses accusation for her own purposes, and Mary Warren, a timid girl who is overwhelmed by the great prominence she gains simply by accusing people of greater stature in the community. Mary's transformation is more interesting than Abigail's because she is a basically good, honest person who struggles against the power that the trials suddenly give her. In his revision of the play, Miller pays much more attention to Mary than Abigail, precisely because he wants to show how good men, even when wanting to do right, yield to the pressure of the group. . . .

Negative Response

Miller felt that both the audience and the critics were very uncomfortable with the theme of witch-hunting in the McCarthy era. *The Crucible* opened to polite, lukewarm reviews; "it got respectful notices, the kind that bury you decently," and after a run of a few months it closed. The play was very popular in Europe, however, and Miller was planning to attend the Brussels opening in 1954 when he was denied a passport by the State Department. The denial of the passport was just the beginning of Miller's troubles with the government over his alleged leftist sympathies. *The Crucible* was revived Off Broadway in 1958 to glowing praise from the same critics who yawned over it five years earlier. This production ran for more than six hundred performances and established *The Crucible* as the second most popular play in the Miller canon. . . .

Miller and the Courts

In 1955, Miller was divorced from Mary Grace Slattery, and in the same year his troubles because of his leftist interests began in earnest. He had been working with the New York Youth Board on a film about juvenile delinquents when the American Legion and the Catholic War Veterans applied pressure to have the project dropped because of Miller's "Communist ties." He had, after all, been refused a passport the previous year as a "person believed to be supporting the Communist movement." The pressure by the two groups was successful and work on the film ceased.

Two years later, Miller was called before Representative Francis Walter's Committee on Un-American Activities. Miller chatted amiably with the committee members about his opinions on [poet] Ezra Pound, [director] Elia Kazan, [author] Howard Fast, Red China, and the repeal of the Smith Act, the 1940 law that made it a federal offense to advocate violent overthrow of the government or to be a member of any group devoted to such advocacy. The committee was most cordial in discussing these matters with Miller, but then asked Miller about his attendance at a meeting of Communist writers in 1947. Miller refused to take the Fifth Amendment [refusing to answer questions because the answers may be self-incriminating] and freely admitted that he had been at the meeting, though he denied ever being a member of the Communist party. The committee then asked him to name other writers who were there. At this point, Miller, like Proctor in *The Crucible*, said that his conscience would not permit him to name any others. Since the committee already knew from other sources who had attended the meeting, it is clear that the questions were asked to see if Miller would implicate his colleagues. Proctor's judges too were not so much interested in knowing the names, but in having Proctor betray his fellows.

Because of his refusal to answer the committee's questions, Miller was put on trial for contempt of Congress. The judge decided that Miller's motives were commendable, but that his position was legally indefensible, and he found Miller guilty on two counts of contempt. Miller's sentencing was deferred pending an appeal. In the following year, 1958, Miller's conviction was overturned on a technicality by the U.S. Court of Appeals. . . .

Although his work of the last decade [the 1970s] has not matched the great creative surge of the late 1940s and early 1950s, Miller in his later plays continues to investigate complex moral decisions, where each man must weigh his individual conscience against the laws of the society in which he lives. That society may be made up of a nation, a community, or a family, and the hero may concur with its laws generally, yet his beliefs will be tested to a point where external verities no longer provide a useful absolute. At this point the hero must rely on his conscience. This is no easy decision and the choice made by conscience may be wrong, but Miller applauds the man who has the courage to make that choice. In his personal life as well as in his writings, Miller has never wavered from this belief.

The Birth of a Writer and a Radical

Robert Hogan

Robert Hogan (1930–1999) was a playwright, critic, and pub-lisher, who retired after a long career as an English professor at the University of Delaware. He was the founder of Proscenium Press, a publisher of plays, books, and magazines.

In the following excerpt, Robert Hogan provides the reader with details about Arthur Miller's birth as a social writer involved lit-erarily and personally in the fight for justice. Miller's awareness of profound philosophical questions and his inspiration to write was sparked, not only by his youth during the Depression, but also by the works of Russian writer, Fyodor Dostoyevsky. Al-though Miller supported himself with a wide variety of jobs as a youth, even before he entered the University of Michigan, he was firm in his calling as a writer. His greatest original works before The Crucible *were* All My Sons *and his masterpiece,* Death of a Salesman.

Arthur Miller was born on October 17, 1915, in the Harlem section of Manhattan. His father was a prosperous manu-facturer, and his mother, herself the daughter of a manufac-turer, had been a teacher in the public school that Miller at-tended in Harlem. Miller was such a poor student that, although his teachers looked him up in their records after he had become a notable playwright, none of them could actu-ally remember him. He failed many subjects, including algebra three times. He was more interested in sports than in school, and later remarked, "Until the age of seventeen I can safely say that I never read a book weightier than *Tom Swift*, and *Rover Boys*, and only verged on literature with some of Dickens."

Robert Hogan, "Arthur Miller," *American Writers. A Collection of Literary Biographies*, New York, NY: Charles Scribner's Sons, 1974. Copyright © 1974 University of Minne-sota. Reproduced by permission of Gale, a part of Cengage Learning.

A Writer Is Born

The family fortunes having been lost in the [stock market] crash of 1929, Miller went to work after high school in an automobile parts warehouse on Tenth Avenue in Manhattan. During this time he picked up a copy of *The Brothers Karamazov* under the impression that it was a detective story and read it on the subway to and from work. The book made such an impact upon him that he determined to be a writer, and for two and a half years he saved thirteen dollars a week from his fifteen-dollar salary in order to finance a year in college. Finally, after some eloquent letter writing on his part, he was admitted to the University of Michigan as a journalism student. He managed to maintain himself in college by a small salary as night editor of the *Michigan Daily*, by aid from the National Youth Administration, and by an occasional prize won by his writing. In college he began to write plays and twice won Michigan's Avery Hopwood Award. One of these prize plays, *The Grass Still Grows*, also won the Theatre Guild National Award of $1250 in 1938.

Miller received his B.A. [bachelor of arts degree] in 1938, and returned to New York to work with the Federal Theatre Project in its last months. For the project he wrote a comedy, but plans for its production were abandoned when Congress did not appropriate funds to continue the theater. Out of a job, Miller turned to writing for radio as well as to working in the Brooklyn Navy Yard and in a box factory. . . .

A few of Miller's radio scripts have been published. Their intrinsic merit is not enormous, but they show a freshness fairly rare for radio, and they help to refute the notion of Miller as a totally humorless conscience of his race. "The Pussycat and the Expert Plumber Who Was a Man" is a light, . . . fantasy about a talking cat who blackmails some influential politicians into letting him run for governor. Two of the speeches suggest the central preoccupations of Miller's mature work. At one point Tom the cat remarks, ". . . the one thing a man fears most next to death is the loss of his good name. Man is evil in his own eyes, my friends, worthless, and the only way he can find respect for himself is by getting other people to say he's a nice fellow." This concern is precisely what bedevils John Proctor at the end of *The Crucible.* . . .

Literary Influences

Miller returned to *The Brothers Karamazov,* and found "that if one reads its most colorful, breathtaking, wonderful pages, one finds the thickest concentration of hard facts." He also decided that "the precise collision of inner themes" must occur "during, not before or after, the high dramatic scenes," and that the climax must be held back and back until the themes were properly clear. In other words, he came closer to the austere [Henrik] Ibsenian tragedy whose chief components were a meticulously drawn, real society, a tightly constructed cumulative structure, and an overwhelming insistence on significant theme. . . .

A Social Playwright

Miller's adaptation of Ibsen's *An Enemy of the People* was produced on Broadway on December 28, 1950. . . .

The reason for Miller's adapting this particular play, which is not one of Ibsen's great achievements, throws much light on Miller's own preoccupations. He remarked in his preface to the play that its theme was "the central theme of our social life today. Simply, it is the question of whether the democratic guarantees protecting political minorities ought to be set aside in time of crisis. More personally, it is the question of whether one's vision of the truth ought to be a source of guilt at a time when the mass of men condemn it as a dangerous and devilish lie." This same view impelled the writing of *The Crucible* and this same problem Miller himself had to face six years later when he was called to appear before the House Committee on Un-American Activities. This plays suggests the answer that, when the times are out of joint, the individual must to himself be true. Stockmann, as Miller puts it, "clings to the truth and suffers the social consequences. At rock bottom, then, the play is concerned with the inviolability of objective truth. Or, put more dynamically, that those who attempt to warp the truth for ulterior purposes must inevitably become warped and corrupted themselves."

This conclusion about the corruption of society is a distinct change from the premise of *Situation Normal* and *All My Sons*, which suggested that society is the giver of morality and that man succeeds or fails by his ability to find a home in that society. It is a conclusion which apparently Miller sought to avoid and which he accepted only after much struggle. In the 1940's his view was one of a simple social idealism, and the issues were clear-cut. As Quentin remarks in *After the Fall*: ". . . the world [was] so wonderfully threatened by injustices I was born to correct! How fine! Remember? When there were good people and bad people? And how easy it was to tell! The worst son of a bitch, if he loved Jews and Negroes and hated Hitler—he was a buddy. Like some kind of paradise compared to this." However, Miller was too perceptive a man not to be moved by the nature of his society, and it seemed to him that that society was growing more and more malevolent. . . .

Witches and Communists

Miller is a slow, painstaking, and deliberate writer who sometimes composes thousands of pages to get a hundred that are right. Consequently, his next original play, *The Crucible*, did not appear until January 22, 1953. It was generally thought a sound work but a lesser one than *Death of a Salesman*. In its original run it achieved only 197 performances, but its off-Broadway revival several years later played well over 500. Its merits were at first overshadowed by the notoriety of its most obvious theme. The subject of the play, the Salem witch trials of 1692, was distractingly applicable to what has been called the witch hunts of the 1950's. Now, when the most impassioned fervor of Communist hunting has abated, the play may probably be judged on its own merits, unobscured by newspaper headlines.

The Crucible is a strong play, and its conclusion has much of the force of tragedy. It has not the permeating compassion of *Death of a Salesman*, but there is more dramatic power to John Proctor's death than there was to Willy's. It is a harder-hitting play, and its impact stems from Proctor's death being really a triumph. You cannot pity a man who triumphs. Willy Loman's death was a failure, and his suicide only a gesture of defeat. Him you can pity. . . .

There followed [after *A View from the Bridge*] a long hiatus in Miller's work for the stage that may be traced in part to his personal life and in part to his politics. Several of his plays had been attacked by organizations of the far right for their alleged Communist leanings (the same plays had run into trouble in Russia because of their alleged capitalist leanings), but his trouble with his own government really began when the State Department in 1954 refused him a passport "as a person believed to be supporting the Communist movement." His name was blackened somewhat more in 1955 when he was preparing a film scenario about the work of the New York Youth Board with juvenile delinquents. The American Legion and the Catholic War Veterans so strenuously objected to Miller on the basis of his alleged Communist sympathies that the film was ultimately dropped.

On June 21, 1956, Miller appeared before the House Committee on Un-American Activities and talked freely about his support of various Communist Front groups in the 1940's, and of how he had attended some Communist-sponsored meetings of writers. All questions about himself he answered fully and frankly, but he refused to answer two questions requiring him to name people whom he had seen at the meetings. For his refusal to name names, he was cited for contempt of Congress, fined $500, and given a suspended sentence of thirty days in jail, but he was also given a passport valid for six months. . . .

About Miller, we can be sure of at least this much: he is one of the five or six incontestably fine writers for the theater that America has produced. His position in the drama of America and, indeed, in the drama of the twentieth century, is both secure and high.

A Committed Activist

Steven R. Centola

Steven R. Centola (1952–2008), was professor of English at Millersville University in Pennsylvania, the founder and president of the Arthur Miller Society, and the author of several books on Miller.

The Miller family's loss during the Great Depression of their business, economic status, and comfortable way of life shaped Arthur Miller's point of view in writing plays about social problems, including the suffering of the individual at the hands of an unjust government and the obligation of the individual to accept social responsibility. His play All My Sons, *about war profiteering and irresponsible capitalism, established him as a leading American playwright. His greatest play,* Death of a Salesman, *showed the emptiness of the American Dream, based on shoddy economic values. After the lukewarm reception from audiences and critics to* The Crucible, *with its reference to the political malfeasance of Senator Joe McCarthy, Miller was put to the test, as John Proctor was, in being asked to name names of those the government was unjustly persecuting. Miller remained socially active up until his death in 2005, speaking out against the Vietnam War and capital punishment.*

Born in New York City, Miller was one of the three children of Isidore Miller, a Polish immigrant who made a fortune in the garment industry, and Augusta (Barnett) Miller, a schoolteacher.

Miller's Family and Early Years

Miller's father provided his family with a luxurious lifestyle until his business failed at the start of the Great Depression. This sudden collapse of the familiar world was a crucial experience in Miller's life, and he would later frequently draw on the tensions that were created by that severe economic crisis in his writings. Also, his father's meteoric rise and fall and the corresponding impact on the family became the basis for the playwright's repeated exploration of the volatile dynamics of father-son relationships.

From his mother, whose parents also had emigrated from Poland, Miller learned to value high culture, education, and the power of the written word. Miller's older brother, Kermit, was a stronger student and better athlete than his younger brother in their early years. Their sister, Joan, was the youngest and enjoyed her father's favor as a child. She, too, would make a career in the theater, becoming an accomplished actress under the stage name Joan Copeland.

After Isidore Miller's business failed, the family moved from Manhattan to Brooklyn, where Miller attended high school while living among relatives and family friends, who would become a source of inspiration for much of his early drama, particularly the Loman family tragedy in *Death of a Salesman*. Miller did not distinguish himself academically at Abraham Lincoln High School, where he failed algebra several times and was better known for his prowess on the football field than for his grades. After graduating in 1932, he attended evening classes at the City College of New York and worked various jobs until gaining acceptance at the University of Michigan in 1934. There, in addition to engaging in occasional journalistic efforts, he effectively launched his playwriting career; by the time he graduated with a BA [bachelor of arts degree] in 1938, he had seen his own dramas performed and had received several honors. . . .

The Beginning of a Radical Career

Before rising on the stage, Miller decided to try his hand with another genre, publishing the novel *Focus* in 1945. This book holds great historical significance as one of the first American novels to deal directly with anti-Semitism in America. In addressing social injustice and the need for individuals to accept responsibility for the welfare of others, Miller laid the foundation for a continued exploration of these thematic issues.

Two years later, Miller's return to playwriting paid off, with *All My Sons* winning both the Donaldson Award and the New York Drama Critics' Circle Award as the best play of 1947. Examining the crisis that occurs within a family when the father's involvement in war-profiteering crimes during World War II is divulged, *All My Sons* powerfully addresses the problem of social irresponsibility and the myth of privatism in American society. Through the production of *All My Sons*, Miller began a very successful collaboration with Elia Kazan, one of America's premier directors. Their friendship would result in the immensely successful production of *Death of a Salesman* in 1949 but would eventually undergo a severe strain over the question of whether to testify before and provide names to the House Un-American Activities Committee.

After *All My Sons* established Miller as a leading playwright of the day, his next drama not only gained him international fame and fortune but also secured his lasting place as one of the greatest writers of the twentieth century. . . .

Social Issues

Following his huge success with *Death of a Salesman*, Miller adapted Henrik Ibsen's *Enemy of the People* for the American stage in response to the purges of Communists and Communist sympathizers led by Senator Joseph McCarthy (R-WI)[republican senator from Wisconsin] and carried out by the House Un-American Activities Committee. Miller's adaptation was coldly received. His next play would suffer the same fate, as fear of persecution prevented critics from responding positively to his extraordinary portrayal of the 1962 Salem witchcraft trials in *The Crucible* (1953). Once again commenting on the harmful impact of McCarthyism on

American society, Miller constructed a drama establishing parallels between the Puritanical hysteria that brought about the deaths of innocent people and the crusade against Communism that brought about mindless conformity, the virtual abolishment of free speech, and the widespread intolerance of differences. . . .

Miller faced perhaps his biggest crisis as a public artist when he was subpoenaed to testify before the House Un-American Activities Committee in 1956. Unlike Kazan, who voluntarily cooperated with the committee, Miller refused to provide names and insisted that he would not do or say anything to bring harm upon another person. Held in contempt of Congress, Miller was fined and sentenced to jail, but upon appeal, an upper court reversed the decision. Miller's courageous act of defiance seemed to imitate his own character's heroic behavior in *The Crucible*. From this time until his death [in 2005], Miller remained a staunch opponent of censorship and a vocal political activist on many societal issues.

Later Activism

In 1965 Miller was elected president of the writers' association International PEN, and in this capacity, as well as for many years after his term expired, he traveled to countries where dissident writers were incarcerated as political prisoners and petitioned their governments to release them. Until he died, Miller remained active politically, frequently writing opinion pieces for the *New York Times*, on issues ranging from the Vietnam War to school prayer to capital punishment, and serving as a delegate to the Democratic National Convention in 1968 and 1972.

Meanwhile, Miller wrote many new plays, continuing his experimentation with dramatic form and his search for answers to life's most challenging and disturbing questions. After covering the Frankfurt war crimes trials for the *New York Herald Tribune* in 1964, Miller addressed the horrors of the Holocaust in *After the Fall* and *Incident at Vichy*, which were staged at the newly opened Lincoln Center, in New York City, in 1964. These plays emphasized the transcendent importance of acts of forgiveness and of commitments to social responsibility. These themes would also resonate powerfully in his television screenplay *Playing for Time* (1980) and in his play *Broken Glass* (1994). . . .

Miller can be viewed as the quintessential American playwright, as his impressive body of work by and large directly explores themes and situations that are deeply rooted in the American experience. Miller primarily centered his drama on the family and examined the impact of external pressures on the individual in American society. Whether that pressure derived from cultural stereotypes and myths associated with an impossible dream of perfection or from powerful enticements to embrace conformity for the sake of social acceptance, Miller concentrated on native elements in his construction of plots and in his creation of often unremarkable, and as such quite familiar, characters.

Social Issues
in Literature

CHAPTER 2

The Crucible and Justice

Witchcraft and Subversion

Arthur Miller

Arthur Miller, one of the greatest American playwrights, was the author of numerous plays, which were challenged by Hollywood and extreme right-wing conservatives.

Arthur Miller contends that his writing of The Crucible *was his way of dealing with being suspected and spied on during the "witch-hunts" of the 1950s. Miller also saw radical students, professors, and writers being fired and blacklisted, some driven to suicide. When the Committee on Un-American Activities summoned him to testify, he refused to tell them the names of people he knew to be in leftist organizations. Later, after the Broadway run of* The Crucible, *he was denied a passport to accept an award in Belgium. The parallel issues he saw between Salem and the 1950s are the misguided fear that witches and communists were real threats; the resultant hysteria; the disregard of proof; the reliance on naming names; the acceptance of specious "evidence," such as, in the 1950s, membership in what were regarded as communist front organizations and, in Salem, spectral evidence wherein the spirit of a witch was supposedly able to torture a victim, miles away from the witch's body.*

In 1948, '49, '50, '51, I had the sensation of being trapped inside a perverse work of art, one of those [graphic artist M.C.] Escher constructs in which it is impossible to make out whether a stairway is going up or down. Practically everyone I knew, all survivors of the Great Depression of course, as well as the Second World War, stood somewhere within the conventions of the political left of centre; one or two were Communist Party members, some were sort of fellow travellers, as I suppose I was, and most had had one or another brush with

Marxist ideas or organizations. I have never been able to believe in the reality of these people being actual or putative traitors any more than I could be, yet others like them were being fired from teaching or jobs in government or large corporations. The surreality of it all never left me.

National Hysteria

We were living in an art form, a metaphor that had no long history but had suddenly, incredibly enough, gripped the country. In today's terms, the country had been delivered into the hands of the radical Right, a ministry of free-floating apprehension toward absolutely anything that never happens in the middle of Missouri. It is always with us, this anxiety, sometimes directed toward foreigners, Jews, Catholics, fluoridated water, aliens in space, masturbation, homosexuality, or the Internal Revenue Department. But in the fifties any of these could be validated as real threats by rolling out a map of China. And if this seems crazy now it seemed just as crazy then, but openly doubting it could cost you.

So I suppose that in one sense *The Crucible* was an attempt to make life real again, palpable and structured. One hoped that a work of art might illuminate the tragic absurdities of an anterior work of art that was called reality, but was not. . . .

The Individual Cost

In the unions, communists and their allies, who had been known as intrepid organizers, were now to be shorn of union membership and turned out as seditious. Harry Bridges, for example, the idol of West Coast longshoremen, whom he had all but single-handedly organized, would be subjected to court trial after court trial to drive him out of the country and back to his native Australia as an unadmitted communist. Academics, some of them prominent in their fields, were especially targeted, many forced to retire or simply fired for disloyalty.

Arthur Miller sits at the witness table prior to testifying at a hearing before the House Un-American Activities Committee (HUAC) in Washington, D.C., June 21, 1956. Miller wrote The Crucible *in response to McCarthyism. As a result, Miller was questioned by the HUAC.* AP Images.

Some of them were communists, some were fellow travellers and, inevitably, a certain number were simply unaffiliated liberals refusing to sign one of the dozens of humiliating anti-communist pledges being required by terrified college administrations. . . .

A Nation Gone Mad

My view of things as uneasily "fictional" turned out not to be entirely unwarranted; some six or seven years later, in one of the more elaborate episodes of my experience, I would be cited for contempt of Congress for refusing to identify writers I had met at one of the two communist writers' meetings I had attended many years before. Normally, these citations resulted in a routine Federal Court trial which wound up in half an hour with an inevitable conviction. But my lawyer, Joseph

L. Rauh, Jr, brought in a former senator, Harry M. Cain of Washington, who had been head of the Loyalty Board under [President Dwight] Eisenhower, to testify as an expert witness that my plays showed no signs of having been written under communist discipline. Until then, "expert witnesses" had always been FBI men or ex-communists. Cain had a very different and curious history: a decorated Korean War veteran and fierce anti-communist, he had been a sidekick of McCarthy's and a weekly poker partner. But disillusionment had worn him down when, as head of the Loyalty Board, he had had to deal with an amazing load of letters arriving each morning from people suspecting employers or employees, neighbours, friends, relatives and the corner grocer of communist sympathies. The idea of the whole country spying on itself began to depress him, and looking down from his office window he had the overwhelming idea of a terrified nation out there— and worse, that some substantial fraction of it had become quite literally crazed. . . .

The United States and *The Crucible*

The Belgian National Theatre, in 1952, had been the first European theatre to put on *The Crucible*, an exciting prospect in those times when it was still quite uncommon for American plays to be done in Europe at all. . . .

I had my lawyer call the Passport Division. He was soon informed that I was not going to Brussels at all. It had been decided that my presence abroad was not in the best interests of the United States, nothing more, nothing less, and no passport was to be issued to me. And I had even begun to brush up on my high-school French! . . .

Refusing to Name Names

By 1956, when the House Un-American Activities Committee [HUAC] subpoenaed me, the tide was going out for the committee, which was finding it more and more difficult to make front pages. However, the news of my forthcoming marriage to [actress] Marilyn Monroe was too tempting to be passed by. That our marriage had some connections with my being subpoenaed was confirmed when Chairman [Francis] Walter of the HUAC sent word to Joseph Rauh, my lawyer, that he would be inclined to cancel my hearing altogether if Miss Monroe would consent to have a picture taken with him. The offer having been declined, the good chairman, as my hearing came an end, proceeded to entreat me to write less tragically about our country. This lecture cost me some $40,000 in lawyer's fees, a year's suspended sentence for Contempt of Congress, and a $500 fine. . . .

Paranoia breeds paranoia, of course, but below paranoia there lies a bristling, unwelcome truth, a truth so repugnant as to produce fantasies of persecution in order to conceal its existence. For example, the unwelcome truth denied by the Right was that the Hollywood writers accused of subversion were not a menace to the country, or even bearers of meaningful change. They wrote not propaganda but entertainment. . . .

The Existence of a Menace

Anyone standing up in the Salem of 1692 who denied that witches existed would have faced immediate arrest, the hardest interrogation and quite possibly the rope. Every authority from the Church in New England, the kings of England and Europe, to legal scholars like Lord Coke [Sir Edward Coke, Lord Chief Justice of England] not only confirmed their existence but never questioned the necessity of executing them when discovered. . . .

Indeed, it became obvious that to dismiss witchcraft was to forego any understanding of how it came to pass that tens of thousands had been murdered as witches in Europe; from Scandinavia across to England, down through France and Spain. Likewise, to dismiss any relation between that episode and the hunt for subversives was to shut down an insight into not only the remarkably similar emotions but also the numerous identical practices, of both officials and victims.

Of course there were witches, if not to most of us then certainly to everyone in Salem; and of course there were communists, but what was the content of their menace? That to me became the issue. Having been deeply influenced as a student by a Marxist approach to society—if less so as I grew older—and having known any number of Marxists and numerous sympathizers, I could simply not accept that these people were spies or even prepared to do the will of the Soviets in some future crisis. . . .

Parallels

Nevertheless, the hunt had captured some significant part of the American imagination and its power demanded respect. And turning to Salem was like looking into a petri dish, a sort of embalmed stasis with its principal moving forces caught in stillness. One had to wonder what the human imagination fed on that could inspire neighbours and old friends suddenly to emerge overnight as hell's own furies secretly bent on the torture and destruction of Christians. More than a political metaphor, more than a moral tale, *The Crucible*, as it developed for me over the period of more than a year, became the awesome evidence of the power of human imagination inflamed, the poetry of suggestion, and finally the tragedy of heroic resistance to a society possessed to the point of ruin.

In the stillness of the Salem courthouse, surrounded by the miasmic swirl of images of the 1950s but with my head in 1692, what the two eras had in common was gradually gaining definition. In both was the menace of concealed plots, but most startling were the similarities in the rituals of defence, the investigative routines. Three hundred years apart, both prosecutions were alleging membership of a secret disloyal group. Should the accused confess, his honesty could only be proved in precisely the same way—by naming former confederates, nothing less. Thus, the informer became the very axle of the plot's existence and the investigation's necessity.

Finally, in both eras, since the enemy was first and foremost an idea, normal evidentiary proof of disloyal actions was either de-emphasised, left in limbo, or not required at all, and indeed finally, actions became completely irrelevant. In the end, the charge itself, suspicion itself, all but became the evidence of disloyalty. Most interestingly, in the absence of provable disloyal actions both societies reached for very similar remedies. . . .

And, as accusations piled up, one obvious fact became more and more irritating for them: as they well knew, the normal fulcrum of any criminal prosecution, namely acts, deeds, crimes, and witnesses thereto, was simply missing. As for ordinary people, devout and strictly literal about Biblical injunctions as they might be, they still clung to the old habit of expecting some sort of proof of guilt, in this case of being an accomplice to the Devil.

To the rescue came not an Attorney General's List, but a piece of poetry smacking of both legalistic and religious validity—it was called "Spectral Evidence". Spectral Evidence, in normal jurisprudence, had been carefully excluded from the prosecutorial armoury by judges and lawyers, as being manifestly open to fabrication. But now, with society under this hellish attack, the fateful decision was made to allow it in, and the effect was the bursting of a dam. Suddenly, all the prosecution need do was produce a witness who claimed to have seen, not an accused person, but what was called his familiar spirit—his living ghost as it were—in the act of poisoning a pig or throwing a burning brand into a barn full of hay. You could be at home asleep in your bed but your spirit could be crawling through your neighbour's bedroom window to feel up his wife. The owner of that wandering spirit was thereupon obliged to account to the court for his crime. With the entrance of Spectral Evidence the air quickly filed with the

malign spirits of those identified by good Christians as confederates of the Beast, and with this, of course, the Devil himself really did dance happily into Salem village and proceeded
to take the place apart. . . .

The Crucible straddles two very different worlds to make
them one, but in the usual sense of the word it is not history
but rather a moral, political and psychological construct that
floats on the fluid emotions of both eras.

Religion, the Courts, and the Individual

Thomas P. Adler

Thomas P. Adler, professor of literature at Purdue University, is the author of many books and articles on American drama, including American Drama, 1940–1960: A Critical History.

Arthur Miller admired and had much in common with the Norwegian social dramatist, Henrik Ibsen, whose play, An Enemy of the People, *was adapted by Miller. In the following excerpt, Thomas P. Adler sees this adaptation as a precursor of* The Crucible. *Both Ibsen and Miller wrote plays of ideas, raising questions about the individual's relationship to society—questions that Miller saw as being especially pertinent to the 1940s and 1950s. The key issue is this: When, if ever, is it acceptable for the state to sacrifice individual human rights in order to protect society? The danger comes, as it did in Salem, when the state begins to substitute its own subjective pragmatic morality for absolute moral truths. Salem's subversion of justice by ignoring individual rights and rewriting morality led to tyranny. In this Miller sees a lesson for his own time, a connection between Salem and Washington, D.C.*

Immediately before writing *The Crucible*, Miller, in adapting *An Enemy of the People* (1950), had subjected [Henrik] Ibsen's 1882 play to his own interpretation. . . .

Preparing for *The Crucible*

Apart from the shadings in the protagonist's character and Miller's introduction of more colloquial language, the alterations between original and adaptation might be accounted

Thomas P. Adler, *The Cambridge Companion to Arthur Miller*. New York, NY: Cambridge University Press, 1997. Copyright © Cambridge University Press 1997. Reprinted with the permission of Cambridge University Press.

minimal; perhaps the most significant, given the political climate of the 1950s in which he wrote, is the addition of a speech by Stockmann's brother Peter, the town's mayor, which suggests how, sensing some internal threat to its stability, even a democracy might rationalize the adoption of totalitarian tactics in the name of preserving security and avoiding revolution: "Now, God knows, in ordinary times I'd agree a hundred percent with anybody's right to say anything. But these are not ordinary times." In the preface to his adaptation of *An Enemy of the People*—which he terms "a new translation into spoken English" and which lasted originally for only thirty-six performances—Miller isolates those qualities that to his way of thinking make Ibsen "really pertinent today," chief among them being "his insistence, his utter conviction, that he is going to say what he has to say, and that the audience, by God, is going to listen," and his belief in the dramatist's "right to entertain with his brains as well as his heart," that is, "the stage [as] *the* place for ideas." Regardless of whether this accurately articulates Ibsen's characteristic contribution, *Enemy* is very much in the nature of a dramatized debate. The question it poses is: what is the nature of good government, and, when, if ever, does adherence to abstract principles, either in support of or in revolt against a lawfully constituted government, become an extreme that cannot be tolerated if individual rights and the community are to be protected?

The bureaucrats in power in this Norwegian town, led by Peter Stockmann, define an authoritarian, hierarchical, homogeneous ideal, in which the individual remains subordinate to the state, tolerance extends only to non-dissenters of like mind, and basic rights, such as free speech, can be abrogated at will or whim for expediency's sake, all in the name of maintaining indispensable "moral authority." The radical challenge to this theory of government comes from Dr. Thomas Stockmann, who envisions a more representative society in which those outside the traditional governing class are somehow brought within the net, in order that their "ability, self-respect, and intelligence" can be nurtured. To make his point about an ideal form of participatory democracy ... in which an enlightened electorate is empowered by the very act of its participation, the doctor dons the mayor's hat, his "official insignia," that can, unlike a crown, be worn by whomever the people choose. At this point, he thinks they will unquestioningly support his self-assumed mission of purifying the town's fetid waters, which are symbolic of a deeper "pestilence" of intolerance and suppression rotting the society. . . .

Miller, while insisting vehemently on the individual's "need, if not holy right, to resist the pressure to conform" to society—which would appear to signal a totally relativistic or pluralistic perspective—still remains a moral absolutist. As he writes in his preface to *Enemy*, "At rock bottom, then, the play is concerned with the inviolability of objective truth." What Miller, in fact, found most perplexing and frightening about the late forties and early fifties "was not only the rise of 'McCarthyism' . . . but something which seemed much more weird and mysterious. It was the fact that a political, objective, knowledgeable campaign from the far Right was capable of creating not only a terror, but a new subjective reality, a veritable mystique which was gradually assuming even a holy resonance." What seems most to have disturbed him, then, was a confusion of the relative with the absolute, so that "subjective reality" could be foisted off as "objective truth."

"Something Lasting"

Although it initially ran for only 197 performances when it opened on Broadway, *The Crucible* has become Miller's most frequently produced play. . . . Since increasingly most audiences will no longer remember the particular sociopolitical situation of anti-Communism that reached its apogee in the House Un-American Activities Committee hearings, Miller has made the claim that "if I hadn't written *The Crucible* that period would be unregistered in our literature on any popular level," and that it continues to be the work that he "feel[s] proudest" of "because I made something lasting out of a violent but brief turmoil." Partial proof of that "lasting" quality might be found, Miller muses, in the appeal the work exerts at times of political upheaval, when audiences around the world seem to have taken it to heart as "either a warning of tyranny on the way or a reminder of tyranny just past." . . .

Interpreting the Witch Trials

To study the witch trials themselves necessarily "becomes," as [author] Bernard Rosenthal claims, "a textual problem—one of narration, of weighing competing narratives against each other for their reliability." To a large extent, this proves true of Miller's play as well, for in *The Crucible* there are several texts that are "read" and either interpreted or misinterpreted. First, the playwright himself reads and finds an analogy between two historical texts: that of Salem at the time of the witch-hunt in 1692; and that of America in the McCarthy era of the 1950s. . . .

Although Miller begins his "Note on the Historical Accuracy" of *The Crucible* by stating emphatically "This play is not history," it most definitely constitutes a reading *of* history, with the playwright explicitly rendering his personal interpretation in the narrative interludes—available to readers of the text but not to audiences in the theatre—that he intersperses within the dialogue. In these, he not only expresses his value judgments upon the Puritan community, but also establishes the lineage for those strains he finds still alive in the America of his time. Employing the mythic opposition between civilization and the wilderness, he pictures a society on the edge of a "virgin forest [that] was the Devil's last preserve and home to marauding Indian tribes"; its "parochial snobbery" over their moral destiny—the conviction "that they held in their steady hands the candle that would light the world"—exacerbated by dissension over religious leadership, property rights, economic change, sexual repression, and the movement "toward greater individual freedom," all of which helped fuel persecution of the Other as a way to forestall a fractious dissolution. The Puritan theocracy, in short, had to be built upon an ideology of "exclusion and prohibition" in order to survive. Those who felt the least rebellion against the Establishment were almost forced, then, to channel their own guilt into accusations demonizing the Other. Several commentators have suggested that when Miller comes to set up the conflict between the Puritan theocracy and the authority of individual conscience in *The Crucible*, he might be distorting aspects of the former in order unswervingly to espouse the latter. . . .

The McCarthy hearings, "profoundly ritualistic" in themselves, become, in Miller's reading of the two historical periods, "a surreal spiritual transaction that connected Washington to Salem." The analogy at the base of Miller's political allegory has, however, not gone unquestioned, particularly by those who would argue that whereas there really never had been any witches in Salem, there most assuredly were Communists to be ferreted out. For his part Miller replied that anyone denying the existence of witches in 1692 would have been guaranteed a short life. . . .

Puritan Theology and Evidence

Stephen Fender

Stephen Fender, who taught at the University of Edinburgh, is the author of books on American literature and Shakespeare.

Stephen Fender provides one of the few studies of The Crucible *in the light of New England Puritan religious thought, arguing that the Puritans had no consistent ethic based in reality. If they had, then these grave injustices (recognized by many Puritans at the time) would not have been committed. This lack of an ethic is reflected in their confusing, illogical language, so typical of Calvinist theology. The defining tenet passed down to the Puritans was that mankind could not be saved by deeds or works, but a tiny percentage of unidentified people could be saved by God's grace. The confusion came in not knowing who was saved or truly good, since this could not be determined by a person's behavior. Theologically, appearance, or hard evidence, could not be trusted. Instead the court and community turn to supernatural evidence and faulty logic and, in doing so, continue to excuse and perpetuate Salem's bloody terror.*

Most Miller scholars have more or less accepted his account of the play as the story of John Proctor at odds with a monolithic society. Albert Hunt, for example, writes that the play "comments on modern fragmentation by withdrawing to the vantage point of a community which is whole and self-aware." In an extremely interesting article on Miller, John Prudhoe interprets Proctor's stance against Salem as the "most 'modern' moment in *The Crucible*" because in it the hero works out his own solution "unaided by comfortable slogans, the weight of opinion of those around him or a coherently worked-out philosophy." Proctor's thought is free of the traditional beliefs of Salem and of the "surprisingly articulate" speech in which the town expresses its values. Proctor's plea for his "name" at the end of the play "is the cry of a man who has rejected the world in which he lives and hence can no longer use the language of that world."

Puritans and Morals

This essay attempts to support Prudhoe's reading of *The Crucible* as a dramatic contest of language, but to question the assumption that he shares with Miller himself and with other critics of Miller that the Puritans in the play have a consistent moral outlook. Indeed, if one examines the language, both of real Puritans and of the characters in *The Crucible*, it becomes clear that it is the speech of a society totally without moral referents. Salem confronts Proctor not with a monolithic ethic (however misguided) but with the total absence of any ethic. The townspeople are certain of their moral standards only on the level of abstraction; on the level of the facts of human behaviour they share no criteria for judgement, and it is this lack which makes them victims—as well as protagonists—of the witch hunt. Their language reflects this complete disjunction between their theory and the facts of human action. Proctor finally demolishes their phony language and painfully reconstructs a halting, but honest way of speaking in which words are once again related to their lexis. But the effect of this achievement is not to break away from the ethic of Salem; rather it is to construct the first consistent moral system in the play, a system in which fact and theory can at last coalesce. Proctor serves himself by recovering his "name"; he serves Salem by giving it a viable language.

In the Introduction to the *Collected Plays* Miller writes that what struck him most forcefully when he examined the records of the Salem trials was the "absolute dedication to evil displayed by the judges." What is more obvious to the audience of *The Crucible* is the extent to which Miller—always sensitive to the spoken word—has picked up and transmitted the language of these verbatim reports, and not only the language but the entire Puritan "system" of ethics which that language embodies.

The Key Was God's Grace, Not Man's Works

The ethics of a society as nearly theocratic as that of the American Puritans owed much to the society's doctrine of salvation. American Puritans called themselves "Covenanters" and thought of themselves as having achieved a compromise between the Calvinist [after John Calvin] theory of predestination and the Arminian [after Jacobus Arminius] stress on works as efficacious for salvation. Calvinism taught that before the Creation a certain, immutable number of men were elected to salvation and the rest left to eternal damnation. Because nothing in the subsequent lives of men could affect their predetermined fate, good works were inefficacious to salvation. The obvious practical application was that no one need bother about his conduct; though behaviour might or might not be an indication of one's predetermined state, it had no formal effect on it.

Covenantal theology tried to soften this demoralizing theory by developing the doctrine of the two Covenants. God was said to have offered man two Covenants: the first, the Covenant of Works, made with Adam, offered everlasting life in return for obedience to the Laws; after Adam had broken this agreement and his sin had been imputed to all mankind, God in his mercy offered another Covenant, first to Abraham, then through Moses to the Israelites, finally through Christ to Christians. This Covenant of Grace offered life in return for a more passive obedience: faith in, and imitation of God. Man must still keep the law to the best of his ability, but, by the new Covenant of Grace, he will be judged by the spirit, not by the letter, of the law. It is doubtful, however, whether the doctrine of the Covenants really altered much the basic tenets—and the practical effects—of the notion of predestination. Works might be interpreted as efficacious for salvation, but still only if they proceeded from a state of grace. Man's role was passive; once he had been involved in the Covenant of Grace, he could perform works fruitful to his salvation, but God withheld or extended the initial, "triggering" grace at his pleasure. There could be no question of a man "earning" grace by his works. . . .

It's Either Black or White

It is possible to make too little of the Covenantal theologians' attempt to compromise with Calvinism; after all, though they confused Calvinism's brutal logic, they also made it more human and, if one may say so, more Christian. Nevertheless, the central doctrine of predestination was left intact. Works are no longer exclusively inefficacious; now some good works are more equal than others. But we are still denied objective criteria for determining which is which. This fact, combined with the notion that, as [Puritan theologian John] Preston says, all men are "good or bad" and "there is no middle sort of men in the world" is the theory behind perhaps the biggest single effect of the Reformation on practical morality. For better or worse, as two American critics have noted, Puritan predestination breaks down the whole structure of . . . ethics sweeping away an idea of *degrees* of good and evil. . . .

So, far from having a "higher self-awareness," as Miller thought, the American Puritans were undecided about how much importance to give to specific human acts: good works may or may not proceed from a state of grace; all that was certain was that nothing was what it seemed; the concrete fact had no assured validity. But what Miller has caught so successfully, despite his theory, is the peculiar way in which the Puritans spoke whenever they talked about sin. One can say even more than that: Miller has, in fact, made the fullest dramatic use of the language, using its peculiarities to limit the characters speaking it and even making it part of the play's subject. . . .

Facts and Evidence Don't Count

What makes [Reverend John] Hale so vulnerable to the witch hunt is not—as with the other townspeople—his repressed emotions, but his love of abstraction. Hale, like any other educated Puritan, discounts the obvious. The concrete fact is not to be trusted. Thus at his first entrance, he recognizes Rebecca Nurse without having been introduced to her because she looks "as such a good soul should." But later, when he begins to apply his theories to the problem of Salem, he tells the Proctors "it is possible" that Rebecca is a witch. Proctor answers: "But it's hard to think so pious a woman be secretly a Devil's bitch after seventy year of such good prayer." "Aye," replies Hale, "but the Devil is a wily one, you cannot deny it." His search for the form behind the shadow finally leads him to an almost comical reversal of cause and effect:

> I cannot think God be provoked so grandly by such a petty cause. The jails are packed—our greatest judges sit in Salem now—and hangin's promised. Man, we must look to cause proportionate. Was there murder done, perhaps, and never brought to light? Abomination? Some secret blasphemy that stinks to heaven? Think on cause, man, and let you help me to discover it.

When the facts become unimportant (and in this case the fact is Hale's "petty cause"—Abigail's alleged jealousy of Elizabeth Proctor), the choice of words becomes unimportant also: "abomination" and "secret blasphemy" mean little to us because Hale himself is unsure of what he means by them.

[Judge] Danforth, too, has his pseudo precision:

> . . . you must understand, sir, that a person is either with this court or he must be counted against it, there be no road

between. This is a sharp time, now, a precise time—we no longer live in the dusky afternoon when evil mixed itself with good and befuddled the world. Now, by God's grace, the shining sun is up, and them that fear not light will surely praise it. I hope you will be one of those.

Either Good or Bad

This reminds us of Hale's catalogue of witches, of John Preston's statement that "*. . . all men are divided into these two rankes, either they are good or bad*"; Miller has made good ironic use of the Puritan habit of constructing false disjunctions. Danforth's formulation looks precise, but misses the point because it establishes a false criterion of guilt (whether the accused approves of the court). So not only is it untrue to say that one is either with the court or "must be counted against it"; it is irrelevant. The trial has now reached its final stage in its retreat from the realities of the situation: it began unrealistically enough by examining the causes for the presence of something which had yet to be proved; then it began to take account of the wrong evidence, to listen to the wrong people; finally it becomes completely self-enclosed, and self-justifying, asking not whether the accused is guilty of being a witch but whether he or she supports the court.

In its withdrawal from reality the court takes advantage of the semantic uncertainty of the Salem townspeople, and, in so doing, makes them even more uncertain. Act Three opens with the sounds of [Judge] Hathorne examining Martha Corey offstage:

> HATHORNE'S VOICE: Now, Martha Corey, there is abundant evidence in our hands to show that you have given yourself to the reading of fortunes. Do you deny it?
>
> MARTHA COREY'S VOICE: I am innocent to a witch. I know not what a witch is.
>
> HATHORNE'S VOICE: How do you know, then, that you are not a witch?

Later, when even Hale begins to doubt the wisdom of the court, he tells Danforth: "We cannot blink it more. There is a prodigious fear of this court in the country—" And Danforth answers: "Then there is a prodigious guilt in the country." Terms are now quite rootless; the syntax suggests that "gear" and "guilt" are interchangeable.

How can the honest man combat this utter confusion of language and of the values which language transmits? One solution is simply to reject the slippery terminology and revert to a more primitive way of speaking:

> DANFORTH, *turning to Giles*: Mr. Putnam states your charge is a lie. What say you to that?

> GILES, *furious, his fists clenched*: A fart on Thomas Putnam, that is what I say to that!

This is one of the funniest moments in the play because it is true *discordia concors*. The audience senses the discrepancy (to say the least) between Giles's level of speech and the rhetoric of the court, but it also appreciates the desperate need to break away from the court's dubious terminology.

John Proctor's attack on the court's language is more serious, and more complex. He first meets it straightforwardly, trying to reverse the distorted meanings of the words it uses, or at least to restore the proper words to their proper places. When [Ezekiel] Cheever visits his house to tell him Elizabeth has been accused, Proctor says: "Is the accuser always holy now? Were they born this morning as clean as God's fingers? I'll tell you what's walking Salem—vengeance is walking Salem. We are what we always were in Salem but now the little crazy children are jangling the keys of the kingdom, and common vengeance writes the law!" Although Proctor is talking here to Cheever, he is also trying to put right a false formulation that Hale has made earlier in the scene, a characteristically imprecise use of a concrete image as an abstraction: "the Devil is alive in Salem." Proctor is trying to reassert the authority of the proper word.

Justice and Fanaticism

Dennis Welland

Dennis Welland (1919–2002) is considered a father of American studies in England, where he taught at the University of Nottingham and the University of Manchester. He has written about poet Wilfred Owen and author Mark Twain.

Arthur Miller's The Crucible *was not only relevant to the McCarthy hearings, but also to other miscarriages of justice. In the following excerpt, author Dennis Welland emphasizes that* The Crucible *appeals more to thought than feeling. Welland also interprets the play as stressing the escalating evil of Puritan fanaticism, which leads otherwise decent people to accept flawed evidence. The play focuses, writes Welland, on the "precariousness" of virtue in a community.*

The witch-hunts that took place in Salem in 1962 were in the minds of many people two hundred and sixty years later. At least two other plays on the subject had reached the stage before *The Crucible* opened on Broadway on 22 January 1953. . . .

Witches and Congress

One of the factors behind this revival of interest was no doubt the appearance in 1949 of Marion L. Starkey's [book] *The Devil in Massachusetts*, a very readable investigation into the whole issue from the psychological as well as from the historical standpoint, which had made a detailed account of the happenings and the trials more accessible than ever before. In the Introduction the author leaves us in no doubt as to one part of her purpose, telling us that:

the story of 1692 is of far more than antiquarian interest; it is an allegory of our times. One would like to believe that leaders of the modern world can in the end deal with delusion as sanely and courageously as the men of old Massachusetts dealt with theirs. . . .

If [author Nathaniel] Hawthorne and his contemporaries saw it primarily as an illustration of "man's inhumanity to man," and a matter of sin and personal guilt, they did not have our reasons for looking at it in the wider social context that leads Marion Starkey to speak of the "ideological intensities which rent its age no less than they do ours," and to remind us that:

> Only twenty witches were executed, a microscopic number compared to . . . the millions who have died in the species of witch-hunts peculiar to our own rational, scientific times.

By the autumn of 1952 these words had been given greater immediacy by the mounting fury of the latest species of witch-hunt being conducted by Senator Joseph McCarthy as a Congressional investigation into unAmerican activities.

Here was an important subject ready to hand for an able dramatist to exploit, and Miller was the obvious man to tackle it. His background of Depression-engendered liberalism, his passionate belief in social responsibility, and his proven ability to handle themes of guilt and punishment, all qualified him for it. Indeed, he had almost inevitably been moving towards it for longer than he had realised. . . .

The objection that Salem does not present a sufficiently precise parallel, because "whereas witchcraft was pure delusion, subversion is a reality, no matter how unwisely or intemperately it may be combatted," ignores Miller's implication that, where evidence is only circumstantial, the dividing line between delusion and reality is so difficult to draw that utmost caution is essential. . . .

By treating this problem in a seventeenth- rather than in a twentieth-century context, Miller sacrifices the questionable

Joseph McCarthy, who served as a U.S. Republican senator from Wisconsin from 1947 until his death in 1957, and from whose name the term "McCarthyism" was coined, testifies against the U.S. Army during the Army-McCarthy hearings in Washington, D.C., in 1954. McCarthy stands before a map which charts Communist activity in the United States. Hulton Archive/Getty Images.

advantage of extreme topicality for the greater gain of perspective. He is insisting on this as a perennial American problem, not merely a present-day one. The terms in which he defines his anxiety reminds us of this. . . .

It is not so much a story of two ideologies in conflict as a story of conscientious endeavour in an uncertain world. . . .

Not What Proctor Feels but What He Thinks

In *The Crucible* the wiser characters do not presume to dictate anyone's duty to [John Proctor], for that would be asking him to hand over his conscience. Moreover, they themselves are too perplexed by the conflicting implications of the issues to be dogmatic. Elizabeth's quietly-delivered suggestions here are the thoughts of a worried but honest mind spoken aloud for her husband's benefit, and he replies in the same key: "I'll think on it. . . . I think it is not easy to prove she's fraud, and the town gone so silly." Far from indicating a limited vocabulary, either of character or author, the repetition of this formula "I think" is in fact a very skilfully-managed way of suggesting the scruples, the misgivings, and the conscientious earnestness which are all that these people can bring against the diabolic impetus of the witch-hunt. It is significant that Miller chose to dramatise the story of John Proctor, the plain farmer, rather than the equally well-documented story of George Burrough, the minister, who was also accused of witchcraft and hanged for it. Miller's invention of Proctor's earlier adultery with Abigail is not the outcome of a mercenary desire to add a spice of sensationalism to the play. It is a similar insistence on the human vulnerability of a man who is not a saint, not even an ordained minister fortified by a theological training, but just a decent man trying to understand and to translate into action the dictates of his conscience, trying to do, not what he *feels*, but what he *thinks*, is right. . . .

The Fragility of Virtue

It is salutary, then, to find Miller enunciating this general belief in the need for literature to recognise evil, but it is a little disconcerting to find it in this specific context. The dedication to evil, of which he speaks, "not mistaking it for good, but *knowing it as evil* [my italics] and loving it as evil," may perhaps be imputed in this play—and we may disregard the sources in this discussion—to those characters who deliberately and cynically give false evidence, or incite others to do so, for their own personal gain or gratification. This means Thomas Putnam, with his greed for land, and Abigail, with her lust for Proctor. Putnam, however, is only a minor character, and Miller himself (as I shall shortly indicate) seems in two minds about the extent to which Abigail is evil or merely deluded. Evil can with much less certainty be imputed to the judges, who, hard and cruel as they may have been by our standards, and even culpably credulous, were trying, both in history and in the play, to judge in the light of evidence of an unprecedented nature. To make them more evil would be to destroy by distortion one of the virtues of the play in its present form. The very considerable dramatic power of *The Crucible* derives from its revelation of a mounting tide of evil gaining, in an entire society, an ascendancy quite dispropor-tionate to the evil of any individual member of that society. What is so horrifying is to watch the testimony of honest men bouncing like an indiarubber ball off the high wall of disbelief that other men have built around themselves, not from in-grained evil, but from over-zealousness and a purblind confi-dence in their own judgment. What meaning has proof when men will believe only what they want to believe, and will in-terpret evidence only in the light of their own prejudice? To watch *The Crucible* is to be overwhelmed by the simple impo-tence of honest common sense against fanaticism that is get-ting out of control, and to be painfully reminded that there are situations in which sheer goodness . . . is just not enough to counter such deviousness.

In this respect, too, it will remain a more important docu-ment of McCarthy's America than would a more partisan piece. The ugliness of that affair, which caused so much per-plexed anxiety to friends of the United States, was not the megalomanic aspirations of a cynical demagogue, but the ap-palling ease with which his methods achieved results. So fast and so wide did the infection spread that it could only be vi-sualised as a force of evil of which ordinary men and women were the unintentional agents and the unrecognising victims. In many ways its moral damage was more serious to those who accepted it than to those who fought against or were vic-timised by it, and this is what *The Crucible* so splendidly communicates. . . .

Our pity is demanded for an adult world run mad. When Proctor turns on Hale, the plain ordinariness of his language, lit by an unexpected simile, a rhetorical repetition, and an inversion of the normal order of two adjectives, is all that is needed to make it adequate to a situation that has already been brought almost unbearably close to us:

> Why do you never wonder if Parris be innocent, or Abigail? Is the accuser always holy now? Were they born this morning as clean as God's fingers? I'll tell you what's walking Salem—vengeance is walking Salem. We are what we always were in Salem, but now the little crazy children are jangling the keys of the kingdom, and common vengeance writes the law!

There are more kinds of poetry, and more ways of attacking McCarthyism, than one. Anything more high-flown would be out of place in this play which insists so relentlessly on the precariousness of the foothold of goodness in a world swept by a wind of evil blowing at hurricane force.

The Spirit and the Law

Timothy Miller

Timothy Miller is a historian of religion. His books include American's Alternative Religions *and* When Prophets Die.

In Arthur Miller's The Crucible, *John Proctor and his family do not attend Salem church. Proctor is critical of the church because they often differed over spiritual matters and Proctor refused to allow the church to interfere with his conscience.*

In the seventeenth century, matters of church and state were intertwined and those who rejected the church often found themselves in conflict with civil authorities as well. In the following excerpt, historian Timothy Miller explores Proctor's relationship with the Salem church and how it impacted the court and Proctor during his trial.

In Arthur Miller's *The Crucible*, John Proctor separates himself from other Christians at Salem by avoiding public worship and refusing to have his youngest child baptized. Despite the warnings of Reverends Parris and Hale, he apparently thinks that he and his family can live and be saved without the services of the Salem church. Since church and state matters were tied together in the seventeenth century, his critical attitude toward the church brings him into conflict with civil as well as religious authorities. Although his enemies see him as dangerous, he tries to do what is right in spiritual and civil affairs, hoping to change the Salem church as well as the court but finally rejecting both. He justifies his actions by the spiritual principles that grow out of his attitude toward the church—namely, that group or institutional authority cannot interfere with his conscience. Like others in the seventeenth century, he believes that his religious faith gives him direct knowledge of ultimate truth which institutions cannot contradict. Therefore he remains suspicious of Salem's church and court and does not hesitate to rebel when his conscience differs from theirs.

Influence on the Salem Church

Miller's historical commentary shows how deeply the Salem church was affected by social, political, and financial interests. Reverend Parris, who typifies the influence of the material upon the spiritual, hardly ever acts unless to protect his position as minister or to secure material items, like the deed to his house or the "golden candlesticks." In addition, he fears the power that church members have to order their own affairs: to appoint or depose their minister, to excommunicate members (as they do Proctor after he is convicted of witchcraft), and to override his request that an outsider like Reverend Hale come to Salem. Parris also preaches too much about Hell and too little about God, and he threatens those who lose loyalty to him with retaliation: "There is either obedience," he says, "or the church will burn like Hell is burning." . . .

Challenging Theocracy

Proctor refuses to be bound by the local or the "central church." He tells Reverend Hale, for example, that he sees "no light of God" in Reverend Parris even though he is "ordained." Evidently, Proctor has experienced this light; he knows that it identifies a minister, but that Reverend Parris does not have it and is therefore unfit. The extent of his challenge measures his faith in the light. He defies not only two ordained ministers on spiritual matters, but also the spiritual hierarchy that ordained them, presumably the "central church." Proctor also confronts Parris, a Harvard educated minister, about what is good to hear in church, contending that he has the right to speak his heart. Parris in turn rightly calls him a Quaker because, in the Quaker tradition, his conscience forces him to question ministerial control over preaching. Since Proctor has no fear of overstepping his authority as a believer, he must think that his religion is between him and God alone. . . .

If Proctor's view of the church is in accord with anybody else's, it is that of the respected landowner Francis Nurse who says that his "wife is the very brick and mortar of the church"; that is, believers are the living members of the church which Christ heads. The Nurse family has, in fact, already been involved in a separation from the Salem church. Therefore, Reverend Parris and landowner Putnam, while enemies, have reason to fear that others will be influenced by Proctor's ideas and that they might follow him in rebelling against the church. In addition, because of Proctor's attitude toward the church, Reverend Hale tests his Christianity, and Parris doubts it in order to discredit his challenge to the court. Of course, after the introduction of witchcraft into the Salem community and after Mary Warren charges him as the "Devil's man," Proctor's spiritual life appears even more suspect and strange. . . .

Subverted Justice and Individual Conscience

Proctor probably did not expect corruption at court anymore than he did at church. The court, however, subverts normal due process by making the accuser "holy." Reverend Hale and Judge Danforth justify extraordinary legal and spiritual actions by claiming that they live in "new times." Some Puritans did, in fact, believe themselves to be living in a "new age," one in which they might justly expect "new light" or additional Inward Light from the Holy Spirit. In Salem, however, the "new" revelation that "the voice of Heaven is speaking through the children" fulfills the expectation. For this reason as well as its own self-interest, the court inverts the moral order, "pulling Heaven down and raising up a whore." If there is no moral right, "God is dead," as Proctor says. Moreover, Mary Warren,

ιgainst Abigail, accuses him of witchcraft. The in-
guilt he feels about his personal life complicates
ustances.

Despite all that, on the authority of his conscience, Proctor challenges the court's "contention" that "the voice of
Heaven" speaks through the children. He questions not only
its ability to determine legal guilt and innocence, but also its
ability to identify, interpret, and carry out divine revelation.
Once again, he opposes an institution that claims interpreta-
tive authority or control over God's will. This time he faces
imprisonment and death from the court as well as excommunication from the church, yet he must try to maintain moral
honesty and sincerity.

After making amends with Elizabeth, Proctor suggests to
her that he might lie to win his life, but she tells him that
only he can decide: "There is no higher judge under Heaven
than Proctor is." When Parris, Danforth, and Hale urge him to
lie to protect themselves, Proctor knows that he can look no-
where but to himself and God—it "is no part of salvation"
that they use him. Since Reverend Hale cannot "read" God's
will for him—indeed, no one can—Proctor himself, not the
church, has the keys of heaven. He therefore keeps his moral
choice free of the court as well as of the church: "And there's
your first marvel, that I can. . . ." He contrasts his actions with
those of others: the divine grace and insight that had com-
forted and directed him in the past shows him how to be true
to himself, to others unjustly condemned, and to God. As
Hale's objections show, something astonishing, beyond reason
and logic, tells him that it is right to die to keep the truth.
The court may see the "marvel," but cannot recognize it when
it occurs.

Three times in the play Proctor tells Mary Warren, "Do
that which is good, and no harm shall come to thee," quoting
from the apocryphal Book of Tobit. The text sums up his position. Like the angel Raphael, Proctor encourages a younger

figure like the boy Tobias to acknowledge the truth in public and to believe that God will keep watch over him. Unlike Mary Warren, however, Proctor does "that which is good," acknowledging the truth and trusting that God will not abandon him. Consequently, he finds some "shred of goodness" in himself; to find any more than that would be presumption to most Christians. Despite the judgment at Salem and the church's excommunication, Proctor knows that "no harm" will come to him—that God will admit him into heaven. As the saintly but condemned Rebecca Nurse says, "Another judgment awaits us all." Proctor's apocryphal text, rejected by the historical church as unauthentic, justifies the only authentic course of action open to him: defiance of the court and church in confidence of God.

Proctor's life and death, like his apocryphal text, shows that his relationship with God remains outside the normal institutional channels. He earns his salvation independently, through faithful actions which often do not appear to be right in the eyes of others. Elizabeth correctly refuses to judge Proctor: God will judge him according to the light he has received. In a way Judge Danforth never intended, Proctor exemplifies the supreme moral courage of one who says no to the whole world because of his conscience. Nevertheless, he does not win his "shred of goodness" by withdrawing from the society of others, both alive and dead, as Hale would have him do through confession. Instead, he carries the strengths of his spiritual life with him into the court, standing up for right in an unjust world; his death hastens the "overthrow" of the Salem court and Parris' departure from the Salem church. His rebellion inspires a revolution.

The Individual Versus the Law

Alice Griffin

Alice Griffin is professor emerita and former director of graduate studies in English at Herbert H. Lehman College of the City University of New York. She is the author of several books on American theater and on Shakespeare.

Arthur Miller has stated that the impetus for The Crucible *was the McCarthy hearings in the early 1950s. Miller has also written that his point was to show how public hysteria, encouraged by government, caused individuals to relinquish their consciences. Many of those accused of witchcraft in* The Crucible *were deliberately targeted by their neighbors, who were motivated by revenge, vengeance, or personal quarrels. In the following excerpt, author Alice Griffin discusses how the characters in the play were manipulated by hysteria and personal agendas.*

In *The Crucible* John Proctor is an ordinary man who achieves an extraordinary moral victory when he is tested in the crucible of the 1692 Salem witch trials. In his struggle against his society's mass hysteria and their authoritarian court, he loses his life, but he preserves his integrity, his "name."

The Political Climate

Miller has stated that the impetus for his plays has always been "what was in the air." In the early 1950s it was the hearings of the powerful House Un-American Activities Committee, which decreed that the American Communist Party (a legal political party) was endangering the nation. Party members, "fellow travellers," and indeed anyone believed to be

Alice Griffin, *Understanding Arthur Miller*. Columbia, SC: University of South Carolina Press, 1996. Copyright © 1996 University of South Carolina. Reproduced by permission.

favorable toward Russia (a U.S. ally in World War II and enemy afterward) could be summoned before the committee to confess and recant his or her former sympathies and to name friends and associates thought to favor communism, Marxism, or socialism. . . .

Miller also finds a parallel in "the guilt, two centuries apart, of holding illicit, suppressed feelings of alienation and hostility toward standard, daylight society as defined by its most orthodox proponents." That the people's terror could be so manipulated by an outside force such as the committee or the Salem court, observes Miller, was due to "the sense of guilt which individuals strive to conceal by complying. . . . Conscience was no longer a private matter but one of state administration. I saw men handing conscience to other men and thanking other men for the opportunity of doing so." Miller says he wished to write a play that would "show that the sin of public terror is that it divests man of conscience, of himself." . . .

Subversion of Justice

Reverend Hale, assisted by [Reverend] Parris and landowner Thomas Putnam (who cunningly plants names of his enemies in Tituba's distracted mind), urges Tituba to "confess" to witchcraft and to name others she has seen with the Devil. She names the very persons Putnam suggested. "Abigail rises, staring as though inspired, and cries out." She names the same women and adds others. Betty Parris, aroused, joins in. Putnam calls for the marshall to arrest the accused, Hale instructs that irons be brought, and, as the girls' "ecstatic cries" continue, the curtain falls on the first act.

In introducing the play Miller explains that the theocracy of Salem was "a combine of state and religious power whose function was to keep the community together, and to prevent any kind of disunity that might open it to destruction by material or ideological enemies." But in time the repressions "were heavier than seemed warranted." The witch hunt "was a perverse manifestation of the panic which set in . . . when the balance began to turn toward greater individual freedom." Outspoken against authority, John Proctor criticizes Parris for materialism and Putnam for fraudulent land claims. The witch hunt, observes Miller, provided an opportunity for expressing "long-held hatreds of neighbors"; in the "general revenge" land lust was "elevated to the arena of morality." . . .

Vengeance and Justice

As act 3 begins, Proctor and Mary present to Judges Danforth and Hathorne her deposition that the girls are pretending. Claiming that Mary lies, Abigail even threatens Danforth himself, until Proctor, desperate to prove the truth, calls her a whore and confesses his sin: "I have known her." He charges that "She thinks to dance with me on my wife's grave!" When Danforth questions Elizabeth, who Proctor has claimed never lies, she denies that "John Proctor ever committed the crime of lechery."

Hale begs Danforth to stop—"Private vengeance is working through this testimony"—but Abigail and the screaming girls denounce Mary until she joins with them and accuses Proctor. Ordered to confess his "black allegiance" to the Devil, Proctor implicates not only Danforth but also himself and all who stand by inactive as hysteria grips Salem: "I hear the boot of Lucifer, I see his filthy face! And it is my face, and yours, Danforth! For them that quail to bring men out of ignorance, as I have quailed, and as you quail now when you know in all your black hearts that this be fraud—God damns our kind especially, and we will burn, we will burn together!"

[Author] Penelope Curtis points out that the dramatic impact of this scene depends on the way "the communication of hysteria from one person to another creates a dramatic illusion of a quasi-impersonal force, more powerful and more malignant than its individual agents. . . . What we see is not just 'mass' but institutionalized hysteria. . . . While the girls seem genuinely beside themselves, the outcome of their actions looks so very calculated. . . . [There is] that strange dual impression of incalculable factors in a situation mysteriously beyond control, and an outcome at once monstrous and precise: *a possessed commmunity.*" . . .

The Judge

Although at the time the American Bar Association protested the portrayal of Danforth, Miller stated later that, he had attempted in the third act to show Danforth as disposed "at least to listen to arguments that go counter to the line of the prosecution. There is no such swerving in the record, and I think now," he says, "that I was wrong in mitigating the evil of this man. . . . Instead, I would perfect his evil to its utmost" as "a thematic consideration." "There are people dedicated to evil in the world," he continues; "without their perverse example we should not know the good. Evil is not a mistake but a fact in itself." . . .

When Danforth insists that many have testified that they saw Rebecca with the Devil John replies: "They think to go like saints. I like not to spoil their names." When he is ordered to sign his testimony, he does so. Then he snatches it up: "God does not need my name nailed upon the church! God sees my name; God knows how black my sins are!" Insisting he will not be used, Proctor declares: "I have three children—how may I teach them to walk like men in the world, and I sold my friends?"

DANFORTH: You have not sold your friends—

PROCTOR: Beguile me not! I blacken all of them when this is nailed to the church the very day they hang for silence!

John will not relinquish the signed confession:

Because it is my name! Because I cannot have another in my life! Because I lie and sign myself to lies! Because I am not worth the dust on the feet of them that hang! How may I live without my name? I have given you my soul; leave me my name!

When Danforth warns that John must either hand over the signed confession or hang, John tears the paper; "he is weeping in fury, but erect." Hale, fearing another murder on his head, cautions: "Man, you will hang! You cannot!" to which John replies:

> I can. And there's your first marvel, that I can. You have made your magic now, for now I do think I see some shred of goodness in John Proctor. Not enough to weave a banner with, but white enough to keep it from such dogs. . . .

In the third act, when Deputy Governor Danforth refuses to give credence to any testimony counter to his firmly held opinions, Hale's willingness to consider the evidence indicates that he is both more rational and more conscientious. Danforth's reply to Mary's admission of "pretense" is that "four hundred are in the jails from Marblehead to Lynn, and upon my signature" with "seventy-two condemned to hang." He has "not the slightest reason to suspect that the children may be deceiving me." He warns Proctor, "You must understand, sir, that a person is either with this court or he must be counted against it, there be no road between." . . .

Reverend Hale Questions the Court

Declaring that he believes John and has always suspected Abigail, Hale begs Danforth to "stop now before another is condemned!" He warns that "Private vengeance is working through this testimony!" But Danforth insists that John is lying. [Author] Leonard Moss observes that "Proctor is discredited, ironically, because the lie [of Elizabeth] is *believed* . . . while the truth (that Abigail, the adultress, wishes to supplant Elizabeth) is disbelieved." As John is dragged off to jail, Hale finally makes his decision: "I denounce these proceedings, I quit this court!"

In the real-life John Hale's account of the trials, written in 1698 but not published until 1702, after his death, he suspects vengeance as a motive for accusations: "In many of these cases there had been antecedent personal quarrels, and so occasions of revenge; for some of those Condemned, had been suspected by their Neighbours several years, because after quarreling with their Neighbours, evils had befallen those Neighbours." . . .

Manipulation of Justice

Like all the characters in the play, the devious minister Parris and the covetous landowner Putnam are based on actual persons. Parris's insecurity causes him to ally himself with the authorities and to view the forthright Proctor as an enemy. When Danforth asks his opinion, in act 4, Parris warns: "Let Rebecca stand upon the gibbet and send up some righteous prayer, and I fear she'll wake a vengeance on you." His advice is personal as well as practical: "You cannot hang this sort. There is danger for me. I dare not step outside at night!" From the records, says Miller, "it seems beyond doubt that members of the Putnam family consciously, coldly, and with malice aforethought conferred in private with some of the girls, and told them whom it was desirable to cry out upon next." Giles [Corey] charges that young Ruth Putnam "named" George Jacobs, prompted by her father, the only man rich enough to buy Jacobs's land, forfeit when he is hanged. . . .

Danforth's imagery is sharp and precise; in act 3 he describes his view of the times with those very words: "This is a sharp time, now, a precise time—we live no longer in the dusky afternoon when evil mixed itself with good and befuddled the world. Now, by God's grace, the shining sun is up, and them that fear not light will surely praise it." Ironically, the night and darkness of the trials will follow his "dusky afternoon." He warns Proctor, "We burn a hot fire here; it melts down all concealment," one of Danforth's many statements with ironic implications, for the concealment of the accusers goes unrecognized, even when Proctor attempts to prove otherwise. The trial as symbol and as dramatic device will reappear in Miller's plays, as will his thesis of acceptance of guilt and responsibility.

Timely and Timeless

[Author] Gerald Weales asks whether the 1953 play "provide[s] a workable analogy for the American political situation in the early 1950s." He points out that reviewers "accepted it as an immediate political fact" and "supposed that Miller was making specific analogies." But by 1959, notes Weales, "only the lunatic fringe . . . still conceived of *The Crucible* as a . . . political document. It had begun to lead an artistic life of its own." By 1965 Miller was to comment that "McCarthyism may have been the historical occasion of the play, not its theme." Weales believes that "the chief reason why Miller did not go for a one-to-one analogy between the Salem trials and the loyalty hearings of the 1950s is that beyond whatever immediate point he wanted to make as a political man he hoped, as an artist, to create a play that might outlast the moment."

Bad Laws and Corrupt Courts

Thomas E. Porter

Thomas E. Porter, for many years a Jesuit priest, was dean of the College of Liberal Arts at the University of Texas at Arlington. He is the author of essays on G.K. Chesterton and Shakespeare.

In the following selection, author Thomas E. Porter discusses the popularity of the courtroom drama and how its format allows for clear protagonists and antagonists, provides a venue for the presentation of the story, and builds a suspenseful climax. Porter presents The Crucible *as an example of a contemporary playwright's use of the courtroom format and states that the play's examination of the relationship of the individual to the law "makes the play a significant work."*

Among popular forms perennially in favor on Broadway and in the television ratings, the courtroom drama ranks with the leaders. Numerous television series have used the format, from simple whodunits like *Perry Mason*, [broadcast from 1957 to 1966] in which the trial is a device for discovering the criminal, to *The Defenders*, [broadcast from 1961 to 1965] which used the courtroom drama to present controversial issues in legal principle and in practice. . . .

The Legal Drama and the Law

This format has inherent qualities that attract the playwright of any age: a clear division between protagonist and antagonist, gradual revelation of the facts, application of facts to principles, suspense leading to the climax of verdict. Though the formula has never been neglected . . . it is most favored in democracies, where the Law is venerated and the Court the principle instrument of justice. Beneath the trial formula and the trappings of the Law, there is a complex of attitudes that includes veneration for these institutions. The courtroom has become the sanctuary of modern secularized society and the trial the only true ritual it has left.

The development of these attitudes toward the Law and its ritual began early in American history. Our society from its beginnings had a respect for, and confidence in, the Law. Tom Paine, in *Common Sense*, voiced an ideal which, though it has been variously interpreted, has retained its fascination for the American mind:

> But where say some is the King of America? I'll tell you Friend he reigns above; and doth not make havoc of mankind like the Royal Brute of Great Britain. Yet that we may not appear to be defective even in earthly honors, let a day be solemnly set apart for the proclaiming of the Charter; let it be brought forth placed on the Devine Law, the Word of God; let a crown be placed thereon, by which the World may know, that so far as we approve of monarchy, that in America THE LAW IS KING.

For the contemporary bureaucrat as for the revolutionary patriot, "government under the Law" expresses the democratic ideal: equal rights for all, protection both for the individual in his legitimate endeavors and for society from the depredations of unprincipled individuals, justice meted out with an impersonal, unprejudiced hand according to ordinance. In the Law, so the democrat holds, all opposites are reconciled; the individual and the community, freedom and regimentation, the rule of principle and the rule of men. As the King is the principle of order in a monarchy, so the Law is considered the source of order in a democracy. . . .

Reverence for the Court and respect for the lawyer is a reflection of an abiding belief in justice and equality administered under the Law.

A group of actors from the Bristol Old Vic Company act out a scene from The Crucible, *Bristol, U.K., November 1954.* Thurston Hopkins/Hulton Archive/Getty Images.

Justice Before the Court and Law Enforcement

One of the most persistent attitudes embodied in the myth of the Law is the notion of a "fair trial.". . . The Law is seen as watching over legal procedures and guaranteeing impartiality by "due process." The general outlines of the procedure are: a preliminary hearing; an indictment which discloses to the accused the nature of the offense; a trial in which evidence is presented fully and an opportunity given to the accused to introduce and respond to all relevant issues an appellate review of both the law and the evidence; a permanent written record of the entire proceedings. The "fair trial" aspect of our view of the Law provides for the protection of the individual from "mob rule" and tyranny.

Another attitude, generally and vaguely opposed to the ideal of fair trial, is the sacredness of law enforcement. As the Law protects the individual from injustice, it also secures the rights of society against the criminal. This aspect of the myth emphasizes the absolute nature of the principles involved and demands that principles be applied to the facts impersonally, beyond purely personal discretion. If laws are not enforced, and disrespect for the law allowed to flourish, then chaos results.

If we look at the two attitudes expressed by the myth, in theory they seem to involve a number of contradictions: the individual in the democracy must be free, yet the rules laid down by society constrain him; a permanent unyielding code must be enforced without respect to persons, yet justice can never ignore persons; the majority must rule, yet minorities are entitled to their rights. . . .

The Individual and the Law

One of the most instructive attempts by a contemporary playwright to make use of the trial ritual and the attitudes that surround it is Arthur Miller's *The Crucible*. Plays like *The Caine Mutiny Court Martial* use the formula in a straightforward way to vindicate the hero's actions or, at least, his motives; in such plays the trial is a convenient dramatic device for presenting the action. The probity of the court is taken for granted; due process is the means by which the defense can insure justice for the individual. Miller's play not only uses the formula as a dramatic framing device, but also raises the question about the value of the trial itself as an instrument of justice. At the heart of *The Crucible* is the relation of the individual to the Law, and the author's probing into this area makes the play a significant work. Miller has described the playwright's art in terms of the Law: "In one sense a play is a species of jurisprudence, and some part of it must take the advocate's role, something else must act in defense, and the entirety must engage the Law." Whether or not this analogy holds true for his other efforts is a moot point; in *The Crucible* he consciously uses history and the trial formula to investigate the American attitude toward the Law. . . .

Good People and the Law

With Proctor are associated the "good people" of the village. Giles Corey, the homespun old curmudgeon who battles for his rights in court, Rebecca Nurse, the sainted lady of the village with a wide reputation for charity, are also caught in the web of the law, the one because he injudiciously wanted to know what his wife was reading in her books, the other because she could not save Goody Putnam's children. Corey manifests the same kind of individualism as Proctor; he will not accept the tyranny of his neighbors or the injustice of the court. Rebecca Nurse also shows a blessed scepticism by suggesting perhaps the malice of the villagers, rather than the practice of witchcraft, is responsible for the evil that is abroad. During the course of the action one of the prosecutors, Mr. Hale, is converted in a dramatic acknowledgement of Proctor's position. These personae reflect the protagonist's qualities and so are related to him in the course of the action. . . .

Between the Proctor faction and the bad people is the official judiciary, the judges and members of the court. The court represents the force of the Law, impersonal and impartial, which reconciles letter and spirit, law enforcement and individual rights. An attitude of reverence for the Law permeates the play. Mr. Hale comes armed with its authority, "allied to the best minds of Europe—kings, philosophers, scientists, and ecclesiasts of all churches." His armful of tomes, he pompously declares, are weighted with authority. . . .

False Evidence

Once the witchcraft scare has spread through town, it becomes the channel by which fear, greed, sexual repressions, irresponsibility can be sublimated into "evidence." The Law can
help create a scapegoat on which the secret sins of the community can be visited. Judge and jury must ferret out the secret source of such emotion and expose it to view. This is asking a great deal of the judiciary; yet if the trial is to work at
all, it works because judge and jury manage to have proper in-
tuitions about human values in a case. So the conditions by
which the Law is an effective tool of justice include an ability
to perceive, through a maze of technicalities, the whole issue
and to deal with it in a humane fashion. The "evil" in Danforth and in Abigail is their lack of this humanity. . . .

In the trial, Miller has dramatized the deficiencies of the
Law in the hands of an evil court interpreting a bad law. . . .
Rebellion is stirring in a neighboring town and chaos threatens the theocracy that Danforth represents. So the decision
must be upheld and the law enforced.

> *Danforth.* Now hear me, and beguile yourselves no more. I
> will not receive a single plea for pardon or postponement.
> Them that will not confess will hang. . . . Postponement
> now speaks a floundering on my part; reprieve or pardon
> must cast doubt upon the guilt of them that died till now.
> While I speak God's law, I will not crack its voice with whim-
> pering. If retaliation is your fear, know this—I should hang
> ten thousand that dared to rise against the law.

Danforth makes explicit here an attitude which underlies his
role during the trial sequence. Though misapplied, the principle of law enforcement is recognized as valid by the audience.

As we have seen above, law enforcement is part of the
American attitude toward the Law; it must be upheld or anar-
chy follows. It is just as important to the American ideal as
the fair trial. When the individual takes upon himself the pre-

rogative of deciding which law may be obeyed and which disregarded, the community feels that the bulwark of order has been breached. Thus the icy wind that blows when Danforth speaks is not the chill of his malevolence and inhumanity only, as some critics claim and as Miller himself seems to think. Danforth appeals to a principle that the audience recognizes as plausible. Otherwise, he would pose no real threat. In spite of the fact that his own personal motives include the preservation of his own position in power, and thus are evil, he is defending an attitude that Americans recognize as necessary. Thus the tension in the position between respect for the Law as such—even a bad law—and a respect for the right of the individual to dissent.

When Governments Go Mad

Christopher Bigsby

A professor of American studies at the University of East Anglia in the United Kingdom, Christopher Bigsby has authored three novels and twenty books on English and American culture.

In the following excerpt, author Christopher Bigsby suggests that the Holocaust was on Arthur Miller's mind as he wrote The Crucible *and discusses how the play is a study in power. He further states that* The Crucible *is not merely a story based on an event in history, but an examination of human nature. It is this exploration of humanity that makes* The Crucible *timeless.*

What is at stake in *The Crucible* is the survival of Salem, which is to say the survival of a sense of community. On a literal level the village ceased to operate. The trials took precedence over all other activities. They took the farmer from his field and his wife from the milk shed. In an early draft of the screenplay for the film version Miller has the camera observe the depredations of the countryside: unharvested crops, untended animals, houses in disrepair. But, more fundamentally than this, Miller is concerned with the breaking of that social contract which binds a community together, as love and mutual respect bind individuals.

What took him to Salem was not, finally, an obsession with McCarthyism nor even a concern with a bizarre and, at the time, obscure historical incident, but a fascination with "the most common experience of humanity, the shifts of interest that turned loving husbands and wives into stony enemies, loving parents into indifferent supervisors or even exploiters of their children . . . what they called the breaking of

Christopher Bigsby, *Arthur Miller: A Critical Study*. New York, NY: Cambridge University Press, 2005. Copyright © Christopher Bigsby 2005. Reprinted with the permission of Cambridge University Press.

charity with one another." There was evidence for all of these in seventeenth-century Salem but, as Miller implies, the breaking of charity was scarcely restricted to a small New England settlement in a time distant from our own. . . .

Breaking of Charity

One dictionary definition of a crucible is that it is a place of extreme heat, "a severe test". John Proctor and those others summoned before a court in Salem discovered the meaning of that. Yet such tests, less formal, less judicial, less public, are the small change of daily life. Betrayal, denial, rash judgement, self-justification, are remote neither in time nor place.

The Crucible, then, is not merely concerned with reanimating history or implying contemporary analogies for past crimes. It is Arthur Miller's most frequently produced play not because it addresses affairs of state nor even because it offers us the tragic sight of a man who dies to save his conception of himself and the world, but because audiences understand all too well that the breaking of charity is no less a contemporary fact because it is presented in the context of a re-examined history.

There is, then, more than one mystery here. Beyond the question of witchcraft lies the more fundamental question of a human nature for which betrayal seems an ever-present possibility. *The Crucible* reminds us how fragile is our grasp on those shared values that are the foundation of any society. It is a play written not only at a time when America seemed to sanction the abandonment of the normal decencies and legalities of civilised life but in the shadow of a still greater darkness, for the Holocaust was in Miller's mind, as it had been in the mind of [author] Marion Starkey, whose book [*The Devil in Massachusetts*] on the trials had stirred his imagination.

What replaces this sense of natural community in *The Crucible*, as perhaps in Nazi Germany (a parallel of which he was conscious) and, on a different scale, fifties America, is a sense of participating in a ritual, of conformity to a ruling orthodoxy and hence a shared hostility to those who threaten it. The purity of one's religious principles is confirmed by collaborating, at least by proxy, in the punishment of those who reject them. Racial identity is reinforced by eliminating those who might "contaminate" it, as one's Americanness is underscored by the identification of those who could be said to be Un-American.

The Power of the State

If it was [author] Alexis de Tocqueville who identified the pressure towards conformity even in the early years of the Republic, it was a pressure acknowledged equally by [authors Nathaniel] Hawthorne, [Herman] Melville, [Ralph Waldo] Emerson and [Henry David] Thoreau. When [author] Sinclair Lewis's Babbitt abandons his momentary rebellion to return to his conformist society he is described as being "almost tearful with joy." Miller's alarm, then, is not his alone, nor his sense of the potentially tyrannical power of shared myths which appear to offer absolution to those who accept them. If his faith in individual conscience as a corrective is also not unique, it was, perhaps, harder to sustain in the second half of a century which had seen collective myths exercising a coercive power, in America and Europe.

Beyond anything else, *The Crucible* is a study in power and the mechanisms by which power is sustained, challenged and lost. Perhaps that is one reason why, as Miller has noted, productions of the play seem to precede and follow revolutions and why what can be seen as a revolt of the young against the old should, on the play's production in Communist China, have been seen as a comment on the Cultural Revolution of the 1960s in which the young Red Guards humiliated, tortured and even killed those who had previously been in authority over them: parents, teachers, members of the cultural elite.

On the one hand stands the Church, which provides the defining language within which all social, political and moral debate is conducted. On the other stand those usually deprived of power—the black slave Tituba and the young children—who suddenly gain access to an authority as absolute as that which had previously subordinated them. Those ignored by history become its motor force. Those socially marginalised move to the very centre of social action. Those whose opinions and perceptions carried neither personal nor political weight suddenly acquire an authority so absolute that they come to feel they can challenge even the representatives of the state. Tituba has a power she has never known in her life. . . .

Proctor Versus the Courts

It is the essence of power that it accrues to those with the ability to determine the nature of the real. They authorise the language, the grammar, the vocabulary within which others must live their lives. As Miller observed in his notebook: "Very important. To say 'There be no witches' is to invite charge of trying to conceal the conspiracy and to discredit the highest authorities who alone can save the community!" Proctor and his wife try to step outside the authorised text. They will acknowledge only those things of which they have immediate knowledge. "I have wondered if there be witches in the world," observes John Proctor incautiously, adding, "I have no knowledge of it,", as his wife, too, insists that "I cannot believe it." When Proctor asserts his right to freedom of thought and speech—"I may speak my heart, I think"—he is reminded that this had been the sin of the Quakers and Quakers, of course, had learned the limits of free speech and faith at the end of a hangman's noose on Boston Common.

There is a court which John and Elizabeth Proctor fear. It is one, moreover, which, if it has no power to sentence them to death, does nonetheless command their lives. As Proctor says to his wife: "I come into a court when I come into this house!" Elizabeth, significantly, replies: "The magistrate sits in your heart that judges you." Court and magistrate are simply synonyms for guilt. The challenge for John Proctor is to transform guilt into conscience and hence into responsibility. Guilt renders him powerless, as it had Willy Loman in *Death of a Salesman*; individual conscience restores personal integrity and identity and places him at the centre of social action.

Despite the suspicions of his judges, though, Proctor does not offer himself as social rebel. If he seeks to overthrow the court it is, apparently, for one reason only: to save his wife. But behind that there is another motive: to save not himself but his sense of himself. In common with so many other Miller protagonists he is forced to ask the meaning of his own life. As Tom Wilkinson, who played the part of Proctor in a National Theatre production, has said, "it is rare for people to be asked the question which puts them squarely in front of themselves." But that is the question which is asked of John Proctor and which, incidentally, was asked of Miller in writing the play and later in appearing before the House Un-American Activities Committee. . . .

Contamination of the Law

The fact is that Miller did not see the witch-hunts as emerging from a battle between old and new money, there being precious little new money in a colony quite as young. There were, to be sure, arguments over property, and such arguments often lay not too far below the surface as complainants came forward to point the finger, but this is not where the essence of the play lies. Miller is, indeed, careful to expose these to the audience. But, in a time of flux, property rights had been thrown into some disarray and authority was uncertain.

Power, certainly, is an issue in *The Crucible* but it is not in the hands of the rich landowners. It is in the hands of young girls who contest the order of the world. It is in the hands of those offered a sudden sanction for their fears and prejudices.

Indeed, it begins to contaminate the agencies and procedures of the state and hence of God's order. . . .

In Salem, Massachusetts, there was to be a single text, a single language, a single reality. Authority invoked demons from whose grasp it offered to liberate its citizens if they would only surrender their consciences to others and acquiesce in the silencing of those who appeared to threaten order. But *The Crucible* is full of other texts. At great danger to themselves men and women put their names to depositions, signed testimonials, wrote appeals. There was, it appeared, another language, less absolute, more compassionate. There were those who proposed a reality which differed from that offered to them by the state nor would these signatories deny themselves by denying their fellow citizens. . . .

The Crucible and the Holocaust

In 1991, at Salem, Arthur Miller unveiled the winning design for a monument to those who had died. It was dedicated the following year by the Nobel laureate Elie Wiesel, thus forging a connection, no matter how fragile or disproportionate, between those who died in Salem in 1692 and those in Europe, in the 1940s, who had been victims of irrationality solemnised as rational process. Speaking of the dead of Salem, Miller said that he had written of them out of "a strong desire to raise them out of historic dust." Wiesel had done likewise for the Jews of the [concentration] camps.

Three hundred years had passed. The final act, it seemed, had been concluded. However, not only do witches still die, in more than one country in the world, but groundless accusations are still granted credence, hysteria still claims its victims, persecution still masquerades as virtue and prejudice as piety.

The Individual Versus Society

James J. Martine

James J. Martine, a prolific writer of books and articles on American literature, is an English professor at St. Bonaventure University in St. Bonaventure, New York. He is also the editor of three volumes of the Dictionary of Literary Biography.

In the following excerpt, author James J. Martine approaches the central themes of The Crucible *through its conflicts, which he enumerates as: man versus man, man versus himself, man versus nature, and man versus society. In the play, the latter conflict comes to the fore, with characters representing society. Through the conflict, setting John Proctor against Reverend Parris, Judge Danforth, and Thomas Putnam, the theme of resistance to tyranny emerges, and tyranny is enabled. The ignorance and greed of its leadership allow this to happen. In a sense, it is Proctor and Danforth who are exceptionally worthy of blame, according to Martine, because they, unlike most of the town's citizens, are not ignorant and do not act promptly to avoid the grave injustice administered by the court. Proctor's early response is denial instead of alertness, and Danforth allows injustice to continue to excuse the unjust sentences of people who have already been executed.*

There is a curious dichotomy to dramatic characters. In conflict they are forced to reveal themselves, and this self-revelation is an important part of an audience's interest in and attraction to the play. It is through conflicts between characters that themes develop. A playwright who sets out to write about certain themes usually has a poor approach to the creation of drama: he or she is most likely to end up with polemic, a work that is preachy or too didactic.

James J. Martine, *The Crucible: Politics, Property, and Pretense.* Belmont, CA: Twayne Publishers, 1993. Copyright © 1993 by Twayne Publishers. All rights reserved. Reproduced by permission of Gale, a part of Cengage Learning.

Thanks to [Arthur] Miller's skillful development of characters, the themes of *The Crucible* are successfully presented. Sheridan Morley is representative of critics when he says that the play is "a company piece about honor and betrayal, integrity and compromise, state and church, home and prison." Since character, conflict, and theme are intimately related, what are the basic and elementary conflicts through which these themes are revealed?

Conflicts in *The Crucible*

Ordinarily, the conflict in a work of literature may be one of several kinds: man versus nature, man versus man, man versus society, or man versus himself. *The Crucible* ignores almost entirely the struggle with the forces of nature. The only concession to it is the almost unnoticed detail that in act 2 [John] Proctor does not venture forth from his home without his rifle. Despite this tiny nod in the direction of the state of the wilderness around Salem at the end of the seventeenth century, Proctor is, for the most part, almost a poet in his relation to the elements of nature, with an Emersonian or Whitmanesque love of the earth, his farm, and its flowers.

More to the point is the second of the classic conflicts, the struggle of the protagonist with another person, and here Miller provides a fecund field. Proctor's struggles with other people are figured in what are essentially minor conflicts with [Reverend] Parris, [Reverend] Hale, and even Giles Corey. His major conflicts in this arena are with Abigail [Williams] and Elizabeth [Proctor].

The most obvious conflict in the drama is the struggle of the protagonist Proctor against society—a force personified by Thomas Putnam, Judge Hathorne, and especially Deputy Governor Danforth. The most profound conflict in the play, however, is the most subtle; the battle for ascendancy of the ele-

A painting of a young woman accused of witchcraft in Salem Village, Massachusetts, circa 1692, who tries to defend herself in front of Puritan Ministers. Hulton Archive/Getty Images.

ments within Proctor himself. It is the resolution of this conflict that will provide the play's conclusion and its lasting merit and meaning.

On its most overt level, *The Crucible* is a play about the collapse of the power of theocracy in Massachusetts and on this continent. It expresses, moreover, the will to stand up to authoritarian inquisition and those who are absolute in their convictions. Miller says that he knows there is nothing as visionary "and as blinding as moral indignation." He confesses that it is only possible to hear, and understand, the voices of those hanging judges "if one had known oneself the thrill of having been absolutely right." Where does the play actually, as Miller claims, send the audience's—especially young people's—minds in relation to liberty, in relation to the rights of people? What has *The Crucible* to do with liberty and the rights of people? The play's most obvious, and to Miller, most important theme is "its message of resistance to a tyranny."

Hysteria and Ignorance

There are other themes implicit in the play. *The Crucible* examines the phenomenon of hysteria and the effects of hysteria. The scenes that conclude acts 1 and 3 illustrate the effectiveness of this hysteria and how it can spread. Miller emphasizes the suggestibility of hysterics; the implications for an indictment of McCarthyism are readily apparent. Once a nation began to see Communists in the state department, in the army, in the arts, it was hard not to see them or fellow travelers everywhere. Further critiquing the hysteria of accusation, the play looks briefly at revenge as a motive for human action. For example, Putnam, still nursing a grudge because of the rejection of his wife's brother-in-law for the position as minister of Salem and the appointment of Parris in his stead, is "the guiding hand behind the outcry." . . .

Ignorance, in general, is the medium in which fear grows. The play explores two kinds of fear—first, the fear many ordinary citizens have of engaging or questioning the social apparatuses that are, in theory, designed to protect them, here specifically the court and a judicial system. Hale makes this plain when he says, "there is a prodigious fear of this court in the country." Fear is related to the power of ignorance, of course, but there is, the play suggests, a worse kind of fear. In Proctor's exceptional speech at the end of act 3, he says that he and Danforth are especially damned. Why? Because Proctor and Danforth know better. They are not ignorant men; they understand the reality of what is going on and, each for his own reasons, have hesitated to place a rein on the course of events. Both have "quailed"—that is, drawn back in fear and recoiled—from their human responsibility "to bring men out of ignorance" For his own private reasons, and in his guilt concerning his relations with Abby [Abigail], Proctor has hesitated to act. Danforth has done so because, as forceful, powerful, and knowledgeable as he is, he represents an office; he is an implement of the status quo, a representative of the theocracy who, knowing better, does not allow his humor and so-phistication to "interfere with an exact loyalty to his position and his cause." He is the law here.

The Law and Justice

This "law" and its relation to justice form an additional theme in the play. Arthur Miller has a devotion to civil liberty and justice—even when justice is at odds with the law. This sense of justice was much on his mind in the 1950s. . . . Even if the judges in *The Crucible* are not lawyers in the sense the term is known today, Miller is endlessly fascinated by—and engages—those moments when the law and justice are at odds.

One of the reasons for injustice in *The Crucible* is that this legal system presumes guilt until innocence is proven. Dan-forth says, "in an ordinary crime, how does one defend the ac-cused? One calls up witnesses to prove his innocence." The situation is complicated by the fact that all of the evidence is not put forth, and is exacerbated because the accuser is "al-ways holy now." The sense that a person is seen as guilty until proven innocent may not stain someone forever, but the stigma lasts longer than might be imagined. In fact, the his-torical John Procter's letter of 23 July 1692 to five members of the Boston clergy, on behalf of himself and his fellow prison-ers, points out that the community had "Condemned us al-ready before our Tryals." While this "guilty until proven inno-cent" is part and parcel of what constitutes a witch-hunt, it may be that Miller touches a deeper wellspring of human na-ture, the propensity that once one is accused, some people continue thereafter to suspect the worst. Perhaps this disposi-tion to believe the worst of a man or woman accused of stray-ing—or even rumored to have strayed—from accepted com-munity norms or mores, is part of human nature; it thus carries the play beyond Salem and its McCarthy parallels to a universal ground.

What Henry James said of the development of his novels and short stories, that character must come before any idea of "plot" or setting and to do otherwise would be putting the cart before the horse, applies as well to drama and the fiction of others. The greatest writers do not merely write ideas; they write of people, encouraging readers to infer the ideas. This is not to suggest that writers must be without beliefs, convictions, and a central purpose, but that a writer, no matter what his or her propensity, political bias, or intention, cannot make speeches without compromising his or her work. The best works of the best writers, whether Henry James or Arthur Miller, demonstrate that. All of the themes and central ideas extrapolated from *The Crucible*'s conflicts are dependent upon character. It is character that is the sine qua non, the essential condition, the absolute prerequisite, to the creation of vibrant drama—and, to a certain extent, the secret to its enduring success.

Social Pressures and Personal Judgment

Santosh K. Bhatia

Santosh K. Bhatia, a professor at Guru Nanak Dev University in Amritsar, India, has published numerous articles on Arthur Miller and is the translator of My Pial Teacher and Other Stories from South-India.

In the following excerpt, author Santosh K. Bhatia draws attention to John Proctor's own culpability in setting off the hysteria, an infrequently explored aspect of Proctor and the witchcraft trials. Proctor's adultery with the household maid, Abigail Williams, contributes to the heinous events which follow. It is Abigail who takes the lead in accusing people of being witches and fans the flames of injustice because she wants to see Proctor's wife hanged so that she can have John for herself. Even though the other girls, Thomas Putnam, and Reverend Parris have other motives for starting the witch-hunt, it is Abigail who gives them such impetus that they continue even after she herself escapes. Bhatia also points out that Judge Danforth finally knows full well what breaches of justice he is carrying out. Still he acts against all reason to continue the massacre in order to justify his previous actions.

The *Crucible*, one of the finest plays of Arthur Miller, can be studied as a test-case to show how social drama is transformed into high tragedy. The social element in the play is not limited to the political parallel of McCarthyism with witch-hunting, but extends much beyond it to the question of the individual's integrity in the face of organized challenges by socio-political forces. Miller, while preparing an adaptation of Henrik Ibsen's *An Enemy of the People*, which immediately preceded *The Crucible*, was struck by this theme:

Santosh K. Bhatia, *Arthur Miller: Social Drama as Tragedy*. New Delhi, India: Arnold-Heinemann, 1985. Copyright © Santosh K. Bhatia, 1985. Reproduced by permission.

I believe this play could be alive for us because its central theme is, in my opinion, the central theme of our social life today. Simply, it is the question of whether the democratic guarantees protecting political minorities ought to be set aside in times of crisis. More personally it is the question of whether one's vision of truth ought to be a source of guilt at a time when the mass of men condemn it as a dangerous and devilish lie. It is an enduring theme . . . because there never was nor will there ever be, an organized society able to countenance calmly the individual who insists that he is right while the vast majority is absolutely wrong.

Social Pressures and Human Integrity

In *The Crucible* Miller explores the nature of relationship between individual and society more closely than in any other play. McCarthyism only provided Miller a contemporary parallel with the actual historical events of the 17th Century Salem witch-hunting. The historical evidence is available in two massive volumes lying in the Essex County Archives at Salem, Massachusetts, where Miller actually went for the material. The play, however, is neither about McCarthysim nor about Salem witch-hunting. The crucial problem dramatized here is that of human integrity: whether or not an individual should surrender his reasoning and sense of judgement to social pressures. In the new kind of social drama like *The Crucible* "it is not enough any more to know that one is at the mercy of social pressures; it is necessary to understand that such a sealed fate cannot be accepted." The pity is that most people surrender their judgement and their conscience to such threats and pressures. Those few, like John Proctor in *The Crucible* or [Peter] Stockmann in *An Enemy of the People*, who do not sacrifice their conscience merit tragic recognition. Miller's own statement in this context is pertinent:

Above all, above all horrors, I saw accepted the notion that conscience was no longer a private matter but one of state administration. I saw men handing conscience to other men and thanking other men for the opportunity of doing so.

Vengeance and Hatred Create Hysteria

The witch-hunting is only a personification of the forces of disintegration which the author has tried to unveil in the play. It represents the web of social evil which the protagonist is called upon to challenge and which ultimately leads to destruction. The central conflict in the play from which the tragedy ensues is between the individual and the forces of society.

The very opening scene introduces us to the nature of evil the hero is called upon to encounter. It sets the tone of the tragedy by projecting an atmosphere of evil. There is sickness and disease, mistrust and malice, pretence and calumny [false accusations]. Enough evidence is there in the imagery of this scene, which is dominated by treachery, deception and lies, to suggest that the world of *The Crucible* is a world where "Fair is foul, and foul is fair.". . . Bereft of conscience, people accuse one another unscrupulously in a bid to avenge old hatreds and enmities. In the commentary preceding the play, Miller, too, refers to it:

> Long held hatreds could now be openly expressed, and vengeance taken, despite the Bible's charitable injunctions. . . . One could cry witch against one's neighbour and feel perfectly justified in the bargain. Old scores could be settled on a plane of heavenly combat between Lucifer and the Lord; suspicions and the envy of the miserable toward the happy could and did burst out in the general revenge.

The last sentence contains the irony of situation dramatized in the play. Amidst such chaos, John Proctor tells Mr. Hale: "I've heard you to be a sensible man, Mr. Hale. I hope you'll leave some of it in Salem."

Our first acquaintance with Proctor convinces us that he is a befitting tragic protagonist. The seeds of destruction that eventually sprout forth into the final catastrophe lie buried in the tainted nobility of his character. He is a farmer in his mid thirties who has "a sharp and biting way with hypocrites." But he is also a sinner, "a sinner not only against the moral fashion of the time, but against his own vision of decent conduct." His sin is that in a weak moment of passion he yields to the lascivious mechinations of Abigail Williams who is actually an embodiment of evil in the play. But he feels deeply remorseful about it and endeavours to make amends for it; in the whole process he is destroyed. His private sin or evil is matched against the larger social evil in the world outside. The outside evil is represented, in part, by Abigail Williams but mainly by the socio-religious forces embodied in Deputy Governor Danforth, Judge Hathorne and Reverend Parris. . . .

Proctor's Responsibility

But the play would not have been a social tragedy if it were to remain confined to this romantic conflict alone. It is enlarged and elevated from what would have been a domestic tragedy to a powerful and disturbing social tragedy. Miller skillfully interweaves the personal and social worlds by juxtaposing the realistic and the non-realistic modes. What appears in the beginning as Proctor's private sin actually sets the whole community in commotion. . . . Proctor's private act of sin leads to social turmoil. Truth and justice are completely subverted. Miller provides the finest blend of realism and expressionism in the form of socio-religious forces that threaten to destroy the individual. In fact, the ensuing conflict is no longer a clash between two individuals; rather, it is a conflict between the individual and the authority. . . .

Proctor, like Stockmann in *An Enemy of the People*, revolts against institutionalized authority. He says, "I like not the smell of the authority." . . .

Irony, which is an important aspect of tragedy, is used as a strong weapon in *The Crucible*. It is the most vitalizing force in the play which augments its tragic interest. In an interview with [journalist] Henry Brandon, Miller once said, "A play is made by sensing how the forces in life simulate ignorance— you set free the concealed irony, the deadliest joke." *The Crucible* it seems, is the best illustration of that statement. Irony is all pervasive in this play and contributes, in substantial measure, to its ultimate tragic impact. Irony, in tragedy, usually involves a tension between the statement and the meaning, appearance and reality, aspiration and achievement. In *The Crucible* it works both on the level of character and action. On the level of character its finest example is Proctor, who has the reputation of being the wisest and sanest of all the people in Salem, who fights in order to rescue others from injustice, but who commits the sin of adultery, with Abigail which virtually sparks off the whole tragedy. . . .

The Un-Christian Theocracy

Similarly, the irony of situation, too, can be seen at work throughout the play. The knowledge of the spectators is juxtaposed with the ignorance of the characters. Irony springs to surface when lies are extolled and believed in and the truth is brutally set aside. Theocracy becomes a farce and the wisdom of the churchmen mere folly. A pack of pretentious girls led by a vile and lascivious strumpet are able to deceive and hoodwink the entire wisdom of the court. The irony explodes the pretension of Tom Paine's statement that "in America the law is King." Law proves a hollow myth. It is not merely the rigid enforcement of law but its wrong enforcement that results in a blantant miscarriage of justice. The law also fails to cope with the irrational forces at work in Salem and becomes an instrument of subversion. People are convicted and killed on such flimsy charges as are listed against Giles Corey's wife. . . .

The Weakness of Reason

The voice of reason is thus submerged and lost in an orgy of lies. Mary Warren, who gives testimony in favour of Proctor a minute ago, finding the balance going against him, shifts back and points at Proctor, "You're the Devil's man!" Proctor's faith in God is now completely shattered: "I say—I say—God is dead!" He laughs madly and says:

> A fire, a fire is burning! I hear the boot of Lucifer, I see his filthy face! And it is my face and yours Danforth! For them that quail to bring men out of ignorance, as I have quailed, and as you quail now when you know in all your black hearts that this be fraud—God damns our kind especially, and we will burn, we will burn together!

This frenzied speech not only reveals the agony of John Proctor, it also reminds us of those dark, mysterious, inscrutable forces which play vital part in the tragic drama of human life. On the level of society these forces are represented by Danforth himself and the ecclesiastical court. The irrationality in their mode of working is referred to by Proctor when he says: "You are pulling Heaven down and raising up a whore!"

The tragic intensity reaches its climax in the last act of the play. By now it becomes perfectly clear to Danforth that the girls' testimony is fraudulent. Parris also informs him about Abbey's [Abigail] breaking into his strong box and decamping with thirty-one pounds. But Danforth, even though he sees the gross injustice involved, persists on hanging more innocent people because reprieve or pardon would "cast doubt upon the guilt of them that died till now." In other words, he must hang more innocent people in order to justify the unjust earlier hangings. . . .

The Crucible might have been timed to the moment and written when McCarthyism was at its peak, but Miller's dramatic imagination saw in the current situation the scope of a great tragedy. The skill with which he developed the theme is sufficiently attested by the success of this play over several years. The contemporary parallel has no relevance to an appreciation of the play as tragedy. It has some relevance to the social value of the play, since the massive curbs on individual freedom and the whole game of hunting for the nonconformists epitomize the larger evil in the society. . . . The contemporaneity of its theme helps extend the historical background to over two and a half centuries and makes us aware of a tragic process underlying its political manifestations. It gives universality to the theme of the play and deepens its tragic impact.

Social Issues in Literature

CHAPTER 3

Contemporary Perspectives on Legal Issues

Governmental Hysteria

Michael Moore

Michael Moore is an award-winning and controversial author and documentary filmmaker.

In the following excerpt, author and filmmaker Michael Moore discusses the U.S. government's response to the terrorist attacks on September 11, 2001, and how it has affected the way of life for everyday Americans. According to Moore, "a mass psychosis has gripped the country," following the attacks and the government has been manipulating the public's fear ever since in order to assume greater authority and limit civil liberties. The twenty-first century's hunt for terrorists parallels seventeenth-century Salem's hunt for witches. Parallels can also be drawn between the reactions of the public and the government in Arthur Miller's The Crucible, *and the reactions of the public and the government today.*

There is no terrorist threat.

You need to calm down, relax, listen very carefully, and repeat after me:

There is no terrorist threat.

There is no terrorist threat!

THERE . . . IS . . . NO . . . TERRORIST . . . THREAT!

The United States of *Boo!*

Feel better? Not really, huh? I know, it's hard. Amazing how it didn't take long to pound that belief so deep into our psyche that the country, the world, is teeming with terrorists. Madmen are running amok on their evil mission to destroy every living American infidel!

Of course, it didn't help for us to watch the mass murder of 3,000 people, obliterated before our very eyes. That would tend to convince even the most cynical among us that there are people out there who don't like us and would like to see fewer of *us* in the world.

Why do they hate us? Our leader [President George W. Bush] knew why, just days after [the terrorist attacks on] September 11 [2001] when he addressed the nation: "They want us to stop flying and they want us to stop buying. But this great nation will not be intimidated by the evildoers."

Now, when I say there is no terrorist threat, I am not saying that there are no terrorists, or that there are no terrorist incidents, or that there won't be other terrorist incidents in the future. There ARE terrorists, they HAVE committed evil acts, and, tragically, they WILL commit acts of terror in the not-too-distant future. Of that I am sure.

But just because there are a few terrorists does not mean we are all in some exaggerated state of danger. Yet when they [the U.S. government] speak of terrorists, they speak of them as if they are in the *millions*, that they're *everywhere*, and they are never going away. [Vice President Dick] Cheney has called this a "new normalcy," a condition that "will become permanent in American life." . . .

Putting Things in Perspective

Our leaders would have us believe this is a guerrilla war, fought by thousands of foreign terrorist-soldiers hidden on our soil. But this is *not* what is taking place, and it is time to do a reality check. Americans are rarely targets of international terrorism, and almost never on U.S. soil.

In the year 2000, your chance as an American of being killed in a terrorist attack in the United States was exactly *zero*. In 2002, your chance of dying in a terrorist incident was, again, ZERO. And in 2003, as of this writing, the total number of people to die in the United States from acts of terror? Zero. Even in the tragic year of 2001, your chance as an American of dying in an act of terrorism in this country was 1 in 100,000.

In 2001, you had a greater chance of dying from the flu or pneumonia (1 in 4,500), from taking your own life (1 in 9,200), being a homicide victim (1 in 14,000), or riding in a car (1 in 6,500). But no one freaked out over the possibility of being killed every time you drove in your dangerous car to buy a heart-disease-inducing doughnut from a coughing teenager. The suicide rate alone means that YOU were a greater danger to yourself than any terrorist. All these causes of death were far greater than the terrorism, but there were no laws passed, no countries bombed, no emergency expenditures of billions of dollars per month, no National Guard units dispatched, no orange alerts and no non-stop tickers scrolling details across the bottom of CNN to send us in a panic over them. There was no response from the public but indifference and denial, or, at best, an acceptance that these tragedies were just part of life.

But when multiple deaths happen at the same time, with such viciousness, and on live TV, no rationalization with statistics like those above can undo the visceral response of witnessing actual horror as we did on September 11. We have come to believe that we are in harm's way, *that any of us anywhere in this vast country could die at any time.* Never mind that the chances of that happening are virtually *nil.* A mass psychosis has gripped the country; I'm part of it, you're part of it, and even high-ranking generals who now weep openly are part of it. . . .

Manipulation Through Fear

Fear, the rational kind, is a critical part of our ability to survive. Sensing real danger and acting appropriately is an instinct that has served our species well throughout the millennia.

But *irrational* fear is a killer. It throws off our survival compass. It makes us reach for a gun when we hear a noise in the middle of the night (and you end up shooting your wife who was just on her way to the bathroom). It makes us not want to live near someone of another race. And it allows us to willingly give up the civil liberties we have enjoyed for more than 200 years, simply because our "leader" tells us there is a "terrorist threat."

Fear is so basic and yet so easy to manipulate that it has become both our best friend and our worst enemy. And when it is used as a weapon against us, it has the ability to destroy much of what we have come to love about life in the United States of America.

According to the Bush administration, and the stories they have planted in the media, the terrorists are *everywhere*. Each day seems to bring a new warning. A new alert! *A new threat!* ...

What really gets to me is the way this band of deceivers has used September 11 as the excuse for *everything*. It's no longer just to pass measures to protect us from a "terrorist threat." September 11 is now *the* answer. It is the manna from heaven the right has always prayed for. Want a new weapons system? Have to have it! Why? Well ... 9/11! Want to relax the pollution laws? It's a must! Why? 9/11! Want to outlaw abortion? Absolutely! Why? 9/11! What does 9/11 have to do with abortion? Hey, why are you questioning the government? Someone call the FBI!

To the rest of the world, it looks like we've gone mad. People in most other countries have been living with acts of terrorism for years, some for decades. What do they do? Well, they don't go crazy with fear. The average German doesn't stock up on duct tape or stop using the subway. They just learned to live with it. Shit happens.

But what do we do? We invent color-coded threat charts. We frisk ninety-year-olds in wheelchairs. We attack the Bill of

Rights. Yeah, that'll show those terrorists! Let's dismantle our way of life so they won't have to blow it up.

This makes no sense.

None of this is to say that certain rational precautions shouldn't be taken to prevent those few acts of terror that do occur. . . .

Who Are the Real Terrorists?

I've always thought it was interesting that the mass murder of September 11 was allegedly committed by a multi-millionaire. We always say it was committed by a "terrorist" or by an "Islamic fundamentalist" or an "Arab," but we never define [al Qaeda leader] Osama [bin Laden] by his rightful title: multi-millionaire. Why have we never read a headline saying, "3,000 Killed by Multi-Millionaire"? It would be a correct headline, would it not? No part of it is untrue—Osama bin Laden has assets totaling at least $30 million; he is a multi-millionaire. So why isn't that the way we see this person?. . . Why didn't that become the reason for profiling potential terrorists? Instead of rounding up suspicious Arabs, why don't we say, "Oh my God, a multi-millionaire killed 3,000 people! Round up the multi-millionaires! Throw them all in jail! No charges! No trials! Deport the millionaires!!"

We need protection from our own multi-millionaire, corporate terrorists, the ones who rip off our old-age pensions, destroy the environment, deplete irreplaceable fossil fuels in the name of profit, deny us our right to universal health care, take peoples' jobs away whenever the mood hits them. What do you call a 19 percent increase in the homeless and the hungry from 2001 to 2002? Are these not acts of terrorism? Do they not cost lives? Is it not all part of a calculated plan to inflict pain on the poor and the working poor, just so that a few rich men can get even richer?

We have our own "terrorists" to deal with, and we need our entire focus returned to them so that we can one day live in a country where the people once again pick the president, a country where the wealthy learn that they have to pay for their actions. A free country, a safe country, a peaceful country that genuinely shares its riches with the less fortunate around the world, a country that believes in everyone getting a fair shake, and where fear is seen as the only thing we truly need to fear.

Homegrown Hysteria

Nat Parry

Nat Parry is a writer for Consortiumnews.com and coauthor of
Neck Deep: The Disastrous Presidency of George W. Bush.

*In the following selection, author Nat Parry analyzes a counter-
terrorism report by the New York Police Department (NYPD).
The report claims that it is difficult for U.S. authorities to identify homegrown terrorists and that it is necessary for them to
have greater authority for surveillance. Parry challenges the report for focusing entirely on American Muslims as potential
threats, and its failure to take into account threats posed by
alienated white males, like the Oklahoma-city bomber Timothy
McVeigh, and inner-city gangs. Similarities may be drawn between Arthur Miller's* The Crucible *and the NYPD's report. In
both, hysteria fueled government actions and civil liberties were
curtailed.*

An influential report by two New York Police Department
[NYPD] counterterrorism analysts crosses a dangerous
threshold in recasting the "war on terror" as primarily a
struggle that requires increased domestic surveillance and pre-
emptive action against American Muslims who might become
"homegrown terrorists" by visiting Internet sites.

Written by Mitchell Silber and Arvin Bhatt, the Aug. 15 report recommends increased police attention "to identify, pre-
empt and thus prevent homegrown terrorist attacks." The report was promptly hailed in the U.S. news media. (*Newsweek*
called it "insightful.")

Hysteria from Faulty Evidence

What makes the report troubling to civil libertarians, however,
is that it lowers the bar for fighting terrorism to simply the

Nat Parry, "NYPD's Homegrown Hysteria," ConsortiumNews.com, August 20, 2007.
Reproduced by permission.

Linda Sarsour (left), a spokesperson for the Arab American Association of New York, speaks to both F.B.I. and Immigration and Customs Enforcement agents about post 9/11 relations between federal law enforcement officials and the local Muslim community. Robert Nickelsberg/Getty Images.

possibility that some domestic Muslims might be influenced by jihadist Web sites, and it applies lax standards to target Americans of a specific religious faith as prospective terrorists.

Yet—except for the fact that Muslims have become all-purpose political whipping boys—there is little indication that disaffected American Muslims represent any more significant threat than, say, alienated white males, right-wing Cuban-Americans or inner-city gangs, and quite possibly less.

Arguably, there has been more reason to fear right-wing militia types like Timothy McVeigh (who killed 168 people in the Oklahoma City bombing) or Cuban terrorists such as Luis Posada Carriles (now protected from deportation by the [President George W.] Bush administration despite his role in repeated terror attacks).

Yet, after angry white male McVeigh car-bombed a federal building in Oklahoma City in 1995, there was no talk of suspending the Constitution or rounding up right-wing militia members for pre-emptive detention. Law enforcement simply tracked down the conspirators and punished them through the normal criminal justice system. (McVeigh was executed and his co-conspirators were sentenced to prison terms.)

Many right-wing extremists also have their hatreds fueled not just by like-minded Web sites but by talk radio and TV personalities, such as Michael Savage and Ann Coulter, who flippantly use hostile, even threatening, language against political enemies.

Indeed, if Silber and Bhatt based their report on actual killings by domestic terrorists—rather than concentrating on a handful of thwarted Muslim plans and even theoretical threats—they would have written a report that not only took aim at violent jihadist Web sites but at hate talk on right-wing radio and TV shows. . . .

The NYPD report also suggests that since it is so difficult to determine which Muslims may become "radicalized," police agencies need much greater surveillance capabilities, a recommendation that fits in well with what is known about recent Pentagon strategies.

A Defense Department document, entitled the "Strategy for Homeland Defense and Civil Support," has set out a military strategy against terrorism that envisions an "active, layered defense" both inside and outside U.S. territory. In the document, the Pentagon pledges to "transform U.S. military forces to execute homeland defense missions in the . . . U.S. homeland."

The Pentagon strategy paper calls for increased military reconnaissance and surveillance to "defeat potential challengers before they threaten the United States." The plan "maximizes threat awareness and seizes the initiative from those who would harm us." . . .

Right to Privacy Lost in Hysteria

In May [2007], Director of National Intelligence Mike McConnell approved in a memorandum to Homeland Security Secretary Michael Chertoff a plan that would put some of the nation's most powerful intelligence-gathering tools at the disposal of domestic security officials as early as this fall [2007].

But the plan has drawn sharp criticism from privacy advocates who say the government is improperly using military technology for domestic surveillance.

"It potentially marks a transformation of American political culture toward a surveillance state in which the entire public domain is subject to official monitoring," said Steven Aftergood, director of the Project on Government Secrecy for the Federation of American Scientists.

Concerns also have been raised over whether the plan would violate the Posse Comitatus Act of 1878, which prohibits active-duty military forces from conducting law-enforcement missions on American soil.

Despite these concerns, the NYPD report lends credibility to the notion that this sort of surveillance capability is precisely what is needed to counter an allegedly growing threat of homegrown terrorism. . . .

Injustice Fans the Flames of Violence

By insisting that American Muslims are being radicalized by their internal identity crises (rather than anger over the Iraq War, for instance), Silber and Bhatt seem to contradict some of the latest analysis of the U.S. intelligence community.

In 2006, the *New York Times* disclosed an official National Intelligence Estimate [NIE], which stated that the Iraq invasion has worsened the global terrorist threat.

The NIE, representing the consensus view of 16 U.S. intelligence agencies, for the first time recognized the obvious: that the invasion of Iraq has spawned a new generation of Islamic extremists who are determined to strike at the West, that Iraq has served as both a recruitment poster and a training ground for jihadists.

"The Iraq war has made the overall terrorism problem worse" since Sept. 11, 2001, summarized one U.S. intelligence official in referring to the NIE, which was completed in April 2006.

The NYPD report also made no mention of a 2006 survey of over 100 of America's top terrorism experts, which found an overwhelming agreement that the world is more dangerous for the American people than it was on Sept. 11, 2001, and that Islamic animosity over the Iraq War is a primary factor in the deteriorating security situation.

Former CIA analyst Michael Scheuer, who ran the now-disbanded al-Qaeda task force, has said [al-Qaeda leader] Osama bin Laden knows that his ragtag band of terrorists can't do much in taking on the awesome power of the U.S. military, but bin Laden hopes that his call to arms can inspire people even inside the United States to take up his cause.

So, if the goal is to reduce the appeal of this extremist message, a logical strategy would seem to be removal of the reasons for anger, such as the Iraq War, the Guantanamo Bay detentions and the appearance of anti-Muslim prejudice in the U.S. legal system.

Instead, Silber and Bhatt essentially absolve the Bush administration of any responsibility for the rise in Islamic anger, at least among American Muslims, putting the onus almost entirely on their supposed psychological shortcomings and irrationality. . . .

Lost: A Climate of Fairness

A 1999 government report called "Who Becomes a Terrorist and Why," for instance, notes that "the person who becomes a terrorist in Western countries is generally both intellectual and idealistic. . . . Often, violent encounters with police or other security forces motivate an already socially alienated individual to join a terrorist group."

By overlooking this factor in their report, Silber and Bhatt omit a useful policy prescription for averting homegrown terrorism, that politicians and police should make every effort to create a climate of fairness that reduces the sense among minority groups that they are facing persecution or bigotry.

Over the past several years, however, the NYPD has earned a reputation of doing the opposite, ranking among the most repressive police agencies in the country. This is the case both when it comes to general policing of the community and the policing of political demonstrations against the Iraq War and other U.S. policies.

The police department came under criticism last year [2006] for the killing of Sean Bell, a 23-year-old African-American, outside of a strip club in Jamaica, Queens. In a hail of 50 bullets, five plain-clothes NYPD officers shot and killed the unarmed man on Nov. 25, 2006, hours before he was to be married.

The incident drew comparisons to the 1999 killing of Amadou Diallo, an unarmed 23-year-old immigrant from Guinea. Four officers shot 41 rounds at Diallo as he attempted to enter his apartment. . . .

Now, the NYPD "homegrown terrorism" report suggests a plan to infringe on freedom of speech by targeting information on the Internet.

The report's highlighting of Web sites as a principal concern also fits with earlier Defense Department recommendations about "fighting the net" as part of the "war on terror."

A secret Pentagon "Information Operations Roadmap," approved by Secretary of Defense Donald Rumsfeld in October 2003, included a strategy for taking over the Internet and controlling the flow of information.

In a speech on Feb. 17, 2006, to the Council on Foreign Relations, Rumsfeld elaborated on the administration's perception that the battle over information would be a crucial front in the "global war on terror."

"Let there be no doubt, the longer it takes to put a strategic communication framework into place, the more we can be certain that the vacuum will be filled by the enemy and by news informers that most assuredly will not paint an accurate picture of what is actually taking place," Rumsfeld said.

It could be said that in singling out the Internet in its report on domestic terrorism, the NYPD report has leant its support and credibility to Rumsfeld's thoughts about countering both "the enemy" and "news informers." Silber and Bhatt mentioned the Internet 42 times in their 90-page report.

But the larger threat from the NYPD report may be that—by whipping up a public hysteria about "homegrown terrorism"—it demonstrates the very anti-Islamic bias that drives young Muslims toward extremism. In that sense, the report may become more a part of the problem than part of any solution.

Misuse of the Legal System

Walter M. Brasch

Syndicated columnist Walter M. Brasch is professor of journalism at Bloomsburg University in Bloomsburg, Pennsylvania, and is the author of fifteen books, including Social Foundations of the Mass Media.

In the following excerpt, author Walter M. Brasch explores the most profound questions of justice in the first decade of the twenty-first century: How is a balance maintained between national security and the legal rights of individuals, and how can a balance be kept between the executive, legislative, and judicial branches of government?

The Supreme Court of the United States has ruled several times that fear and even terrorism might be a dominating concern at various times in the American experience, but that under the Constitution preservation of rights and of law are the best ways to preserve the democracy.

A year after the Civil War, the Supreme Court, in *Ex parte Milligan*, ruled:

> The Constitution of the United States is a law for rulers and people, equally in war and in peace, and covers with the shield of its protection all classes of men, at all times ... and under all circumstances. No doctrine, involving more pernicious consequences, was ever invented by the wit of man than that any of its provisions can be suspended during any of the great exigencies of government. Such a doctrine leads directly to anarchy or despotism, but the theory of necessity on which it is based is false; for the government, within the Constitution, has all the powers granted to it,

President George W. Bush remarks on the USA PATRIOT Act during a conference in 2004. President Bush stressed the need to renew the Act before it expired the following year. William Thomas/Getty Images.

which are necessary to preserve its existence; as has been happily proved by the result of the great effort [the Civil War] to throw off its just authority.

Protecting Individual Rights

Reaffirming the principles of the *Milligan* decision, in 1934 the Supreme Court ruled that "even the war power of the Federal Government is not without limitations, and that such an emergency does not suspend constitutional limitations and guaranties."

In a case brought into the federal courts during World War II, the Supreme Court ruled, "We must be on constant guard against an excessive use of any power, military or otherwise, that results in the needless destruction of our rights and liberties. There must be a careful balancing of interests."

In April 2003, Justice Stephen Breyer, possibly signaling future Supreme Court decisions arising from the PATRIOT Act, explained the balancing interests of safety and freedom:

> Courts, as well as lawyers, ask this question ["Why is this restriction necessary?"] of government officials. Those officials can explain the special need, backing up the explanations with relevant supporting material. . . . Courts can give weight, leeway, or deference to the Government's explanation insofar as it reflects underlying expertise. But deference is not abdication. And ultimately the courts must determine not only the absolute importance of the security interest, but also, and more importantly, its relative importance, *i.e.*, its importance when examined through the Constitution's own legal lens—a lens that emphasizes the values that a democratic society places upon individual human liberty.

The Challenge to Rights

And now, in the "war on terrorism," the judicial system would be required to affirm or redefine not only the precedents that put the interests of what the executive branch called a necessity for the national security opposite the need to protect constitutional guarantees, but also the limits of executive authority.

In the interest of "national security," [U.S. Attorney General] John Ashcroft declared Yaser Esam Hamdi, a twenty-one-year-old American citizen, to be an "enemy combatant" and, thus, not entitled to legal representation, that he could be held indefinitely in secret without charges being filed, and that even *if* a lawyer were to be present, all conversations had to be recorded, a violation of the Fourth Amendment. The Department of Justice claimed the PATRIOT Act allowed the conversations to be recorded to eliminate collusion between the attorney and client that could lead to further criminal acts. However, there had always been a remedy to such possible abuse of the attorney-client privilege since law enforcement could obtain court orders after showing probable cause; what the PATRIOT Act did was to remove this constitutional protection.

Under the same "gag order" governing the noncitizens held prisoner at Guantánamo Bay, any reporter who revealed information about Hamdi's detention could be charged under the PATRIOT Act. "That sounds idiotic, doesn't it?" asked Judge Robert G. Doumar of the U.S. District Court for the Eastern District of Virginia.

The government couldn't provide any evidence that Hamdi had any links to terrorists, although the government claimed not only was Hamdi captured in Afghanistan, he was a combatant with the Taliban government. The Taliban government, of course, had ties to al-Qaeda but was not involved in the 9/11 killings [terrorist attacks on September 11, 2001].

The U.S. Court of Appeals for the Fourth Circuit (Maryland, North and South Carolina, Virginia, and West Virginia), widely accepted in the legal community as one of the more conservative courts, reversed Judge Doumar's ruling, and accepted the Department of Defense designation of Hamdi as an "enemy combatant" since he was found in a "zone of armed conflict." In her dissent, Judge Diana Gribbon Motz, noted:

> [T]he panel embarks on a perilous new course—approving the Executive's designation of enemy combatant status not on the basis of facts stipulated or proven, but solely on the basis of an unknown Executive advisor's declaration, which the panel itself concedes is subject to challenge as "incomplete" . . . and "inconsistent" hearsay.

With mounting public pressure, and facing additional legal challenges, after more than two years the government allowed Hamdi to talk with his lawyer but with the military monitoring all conversations.

The Law and José Padilla

José Padilla, an American citizen who the government believed knew something about the al-Qaeda network, but which had no documented evidence, was arrested by FBI agents in May 2002 after landing at O'Hare Airport, Chicago, on a flight from Pakistan.

Padilla, who had a criminal background as a juvenile, was first held as a material witness and assigned a public defender. However, a month later President [George W.] Bush declared him to be an enemy combatant, believing he had worked with al-Qaeda on a "dirty bomb," and sent him to a Navy prison in Charleston, South Carolina. The only evidence was a brief written statement by a government agent; there was no supporting evidence. For eighteen months, he wasn't permitted contact with his counsel, his family, or any other nonmilitary personnel. The Bush administration argued that to allow Padilla legal counsel would undermine its interrogation and national security. The government failed to produce any evidence that Padilla worked with al-Qaeda or even that he was involved with building a "dirty bomb." . . .

"We recognize the government's responsibility to do everything possible to prevent another attack on our nation, but we also worry that the methods employed in the Hamdi and Padilla cases risk the use of excessive government power and threaten the checks and balances necessary in our federal system," argued the American Bar Association (ABA) Task Force on Treatment of Enemy Combatants. According to the ABA report, which covered the detention of citizens in Naval brigs in the continental United States and of noncitizens at Guantánamo Bay:

> The government's concerns that access to counsel may impede the collection of intelligence, or that counsel might facilitate communications with others, do not justify denial of access to counsel. These concerns are frequently overcome in sensitive criminal prosecutions, as in the case of the 1993

World Trade Center bombers and the current [alleged September 11th terrorist Zacarius] Moussaoui prosecution, where defense attorneys (or standby attorneys) were required to submit to security clearance background checks and the courts have not hesitated to place sensitive pleadings and documents under seal. Lawyers can provide effective representation—and have, in numerous cases—without threatening the nation's security. . . .

While the Sixth Amendment does not technically attach to uncharged "enemy combatants," there is no dispute that individuals who have been criminally charged do have a Sixth Amendment right to counsel, and it is both paradoxical and unsatisfactory that uncharged U.S. citizen detainees have fewer rights and protections than those who have been charged with serious criminal offenses. . . .

National Security Versus Legal Rights

Deputy Solicitor General Paul D. Clement underscored his arguments for the Bush administration by using a "trust us" philosophy, telling the justices, "you have to trust the executive to make the kind of quintessential military judgments that are involved."

In response, Frank Dunham, federal public defender representing Hamdi, countered that checks and balances exist in the Constitution because "we didn't trust the executive branch when we founded this government. That's why the government saying, 'trust us' is no excuse for taking away and driving a truck through [the principle] that no man shall be deprived of liberty except upon due process of law."

If the Supreme Court accepted the government's position, "it would mean that for the foreseeable future, any citizen, anywhere, at any time, would be subject to indefinite military detention on the unilateral order of the president," according to the brief presented by the defense.

"Never before in history has this court granted the president a blank check to do whatever he wants to American citizens," argued defense attorney Jennifer Martinez, on behalf of Padilla. Martinez, professor of law at Stanford University, also argued that even the broadest interpretation of war powers acts did not allow "executive unlimited power over citizens." In defense of Hamdi, Dunham argued, "We could have people locked up all over the country tomorrow with no opportunity to be heard . . . Congress didn't intend for widespread indefinite detentions." He argued that under the Constitution all prisoners have a right to go to court to challenge their detention. . . .

Two months after oral arguments, the Supreme Court dealt the Bush administration a major defeat. In a 6-3 opinion . . . it declared the executive branch could not hold foreign-born prisoners at Guantánamo Bay indefinitely without access to the American judicial system and the rights of due process. In an 8-1 decision on the *Hamdi* case, it vacated the opinion of the Court of Appeals for the Fourth Circuit, which accepted the government's arguments that it could deny legal rights to an American citizen it declares to be an "enemy combatant." The opinion sidestepped the question of what is an "enemy combatant" and whether tribunals are legal.

Justice O'Connor's Opinion

In writing the thirty-three page opinion of the Court, Justice Sandra Day O'Connor, while deferential to the president, and seemingly trying to please both sides, nevertheless firmly stated:

> Striking the proper constitutional balance here is of great importance to the Nation during this period of ongoing combat. But it is equally vital that our calculus not short shrift to the values that this country holds dear or to the privilege that is American citizenship. It is during our most challenging and uncertain moments that our Nation's commitment to due process is most severely tested; and it is in those times that we must preserve our commitment at home

to the principles for which we fight abroad. . . . (The imperative necessity for safeguarding these rights to procedural due process under the gravest of emergencies has existed throughout our constitutional history, for it is then, under the pressing exigencies of crisis, that there is the greatest temptation to dispense with guarantees which, it is feared, will inhibit government action.) . . . (It would indeed be ironic if, in the name of national defense, we would sanction the subversion of one of those liberties, which makes the defense of the Nation worthwhile). . . .

In so holding, we necessarily reject the Government's assertion that separation of powers principles mandate a heavily circumscribed role for the courts in such circumstances. Indeed, the position that the courts must forgo any examination of the individual case and focus exclusively on the legality of the broader detention scheme cannot be mandated by any reasonable view of separation of powers, as this approach serves only to *condense* power into a single branch of government. We have long since made clear that a state of war is not a blank check for the president when it comes to the rights of the Nation's citizens. . . .

The Court Ignores Justice

Justice O'Connor was joined in her opinion by Chief Justice William H. Rehnquist, and Justices Anthony M. Kennedy and Stephen Breyer. Essentially, the opinion continued to put a burden on Hamdi to present evidence that the government is not wrong in its assertions to his guilt, an essential difference from the "presumed innocent" framework of American jurisprudence. Justices Antonin Scalia, a conservative, and John Paul Stevens, a liberal, also concurred, but argued that the Court's opinion did not go far enough to protect civil rights. "If civil rights are to be curtailed during wartime, it must be done openly and democratically, as the Constitution requires, rather than by silent erosion through an opinion of this court," wrote Scalia. Justices Ruth Bader Ginsburg and David H.

Souter also concurred, but further argued that Hamdi's detention itself was improper. Only Justice Clarence Thomas dissented, and agreed with all of the government's contentions about reasons why Padilla, and others, had no rights of constitutional due process. A separate 5-4 decision by the Court declared that Hamdi's detention was lawful; the four dissenting justices had wanted Hamdi to be released from custody.

In a contentious 5-4 ruling the same day as the *Hamdi* decision, the Court sidestepped the constitutional issues to the *Padilla* case and on a technicality declared that the case was filed in the wrong jurisdiction and against the wrong defendant. The *Padilla* case had raised stronger constitutional questions since the defendant, an American citizen, was arrested on American soil and not on a battlefield. . . .

The four dissenters on the Supreme Court (Justices Breyer, Ginsburg, Souter, and Stevens) argued that the Court should have heard the argument because the case presented extraordinary circumstances. In an impassioned dissent, Justice Stevens wrote:

At stake in this case is nothing less than the essence of a free society. Even more important than the method of selecting the people's rulers and their successors is the character of the constraints imposed on the Executive by the rule of law. Unconstrained Executive detention for the purpose of investigating and preventing subversive activity is the hallmark of the Star Chamber. . . . Access to counsel for the purpose of protecting the citizen from official mistakes and mistreatment is the hallmark of due process. Executive detention of subversive citizens, like detention of enemy soldiers to keep them off the battlefield, may sometimes be justified to prevent persons from launching or becoming missiles of destruction. It may not, however, be justified by the naked interest in using unlawful procedures to extract information. Incommunicado detention for months on end is such a procedure. Whether the information so procured is more or less reliable than that acquired by more extreme forms of

torture is of no consequence. The Non-Detention Act ...
prohibits, and the Authorization for Use of Military Force
Joint Resolution ... does not authorize the protracted, incommunicado detention of American citizens arrested in
the United States. ...

[I]f this Nation is to remain true to the ideals symbolized by
its flag, it must not wield the tools of tyrants even to resist
an assault by the forces of tyranny. ...

Dozens of other attorneys from several organizations also
increased their efforts to represent the detainees and keep the
entire process within the federal courts rather than to allow
the military to continue to have jurisdiction.

In September 2004, the federal government finally released
Yaser Esam Hamdi after more than two years in what Hamdi's
attorney called "inhumane" confinement. However, the release,
following extensive negotiations with Hamdi's federal public
defender, required Hamdi to return to Saudi Arabia, to re-
nounce his U.S. citizenship, and to accept certain travel re-
strictions.

Hope for Legal Justice for Detainees

Andy Worthington

Andy Worthington, a journalist for the Huffington Post, *is the author of* The Guantanamo Files: The Stories of the 774 Detainees in America's Illegal Prison, *and communications manager for the legal action charity Reprieve.*

The imprisoned men at the prison at the U.S. Naval Base Guantanamo Bay had many of their basic rights suspended, which allowed the United States to detain them for seven years without charging them with a crime, while also denying them access to attorneys and civil courts. These rights, Andy Worthington reminds us, come under the general heading of habeas corpus. In June 2008 the U.S. Supreme Court granted these prisoners the right of habeas corpus, which meant that the prisoners could challenge their detention. In the following selection Worthington discusses the June 2008 ruling and the U.S. government's reaction to it. The ruling put the government in a situation similar to that of Judge Danforth in Arthur Miller's The Crucible: *it must now decide if it should simply release most of the 273 prisoners held at Guantanamo or charge them and go to trial, risking criticism and embarrassment.*

Those who cherish the United States' historical adherence to the rule of law—myself included—were delighted to hear that the US Supreme Court ruled on Thursday [June 12, 2008] in the case of *Boumediene v. Bush*, that the prisoners at Guantánamo "have the constitutional right to habeas corpus," enabling them to challenge the basis of their detention, under the terms of the 800-year old "Great Writ" of habeas corpus,

Andy Worthington, "The Supreme Court's Guantanamo Ruling: What Does It Mean?" *The Huffington Post*, June 13, 2008. Reproduced by permission.

which prohibits the suspension of prisoners' rights to challenge the basis of their detention except in "cases of rebellion or invasion."

Legal Justice for Detainees

That this decision was required at all was remarkable, as it was almost four years ago, on 29 June 2004, that the Supreme Court ruled, in the case of *Rasul v. Bush*, that Guantánamo—chosen as a base for the prison because it was presumed to be beyond the reach of the US courts—was "in every practical respect a United States territory," and that the prisoners therefore had habeas corpus rights, enabling the prisoners to challenge the basis of their detention.

The difference between then and now is that, in *Rasul v. Bush*, the Supreme Court ruled only that the prisoners had statutory habeas rights, and that, following the ruling, the executive responded in two ways that completely undermined the Supreme Court's verdict.

The first of these—as lawyers began applying to visit prisoners to establish habeas cases—was the establishment of Combatant Status Review Tribunals (CSRTs) at Guantánamo, which were set up, ostensibly, to review the prisoners designation as "enemy combatants," who could be held without charge or trial. In reality, they were a lamentable replacement for a valid judicial challenge. Although the prisoners were allowed to present their own version of the events that led up to their capture, they were not allowed legal representation, and were subjected to secret evidence that they were unable to see or challenge.

Last June, Lt. Col. Stephen Abraham, a veteran of US intelligence, who worked on the CSRTs, delivered a damning verdict on their legitimacy, condemning them as the administrative equivalent of show trials, reliant upon generalized and often "generic" evidence, and designed to rubber-stamp the prisoners' prior designation as "enemy combatants." Filed as an affidavit in *Al Odah v. United States*, one of the cases consolidated with *Boumediene*, Lt. Col. Abraham's testimony was regarded, by legal experts, as the trigger that spurred the Supreme Court, which had rejected an appeal on behalf of the prisoners in April 2007, to reverse its decision and to agree to hear the cases. The reversal was so rare that it had last taken place 60 years before.

The executive's second response to *Rasul* was to remove the prisoners' statutory rights, persuading the third strand of the American power base—the politicians in Congress—to pass two hideously flawed pieces of legislation: the Detainee Treatment Act of 2005, and the Military Commissions Act of 2006.

The Detainee Treatment Act (DTA), which originated as an anti-torture bill conceived by Senator John McCain, was hijacked by the executive, who managed to get an amendment passed that removed the prisoners' habeas rights, although the legislation was so shoddy that it was not entirely clear whether the prisoners had been stripped of their rights entirely, or whether pending cases would still be considered. What was clear, however, was that the DTA limited any review of the prisoners' cases to the DC Circuit Court (rather than the Supreme Court), preventing any independent fact-finding to challenge the substance of the administration's allegations, and mandating the judges to rule only on whether or not the CSRTs had followed their own rules, and whether or not those rules were valid.

In the fall of 2006, following a second momentous decision in the Supreme Court, in *Hamdan v. Rumsfeld*, in which the justices ruled that the proposed trials by Military Commission for those held at Guantánamo (which also relied on the use of secret evidence) were illegal under domestic and international law, the executive persuaded Congress to pass the Military Commissions Act (MCA), which reinstated the Military Commissions and also removed any lingering doubts about the prisoners' habeas rights, stating, explicitly, "No court, justice or judge shall have jurisdiction to hear or consider an application for a writ of habeas corpus filed by or on behalf of an alien detained by the United States who has been determined by the United States to have been properly detained as an enemy combatant or is awaiting such determination." In a further attempt to stifle dissent, the MCA defined an "enemy combatant" as someone who has either engaged in or supported hostilities against the US, or "has been determined to be an unlawful enemy combatant by a Combatant Status Review Tribunal or another competent tribunal established under the authority of the President or the secretary of defense."

Slow Justice in Reversing Executive Illegalities

The wheels of justice revolve so slowly that it has taken over a year and a half since the passing of the MCA for the Supreme Court to stamp its authority on the conceits of both the executive and Congress, and cynics can argue that all of this could have been avoided if the Supreme Court had insisted on the prisoners' Constitutional habeas rights in June 2004. Nevertheless, Thursday's ruling—however belatedly—comprehensively demolishes the habeas-stripping provisions of both the DTA and the MCA.

In no uncertain terms, Justice Anthony Kennedy, delivering the Court's majority opinion, ruled that the "procedures for review of the detainees' status" in the DTA "are not an adequate and effective substitute for habeas corpus," and that therefore the habeas-stripping component of the MCA "operates as an unconstitutional suspension of the writ." These judgments, which should soundly embarrass the nations' politicians, could hardly be more clear, and although it is uncertain how the administration will respond in its dying days [President Bush leaves office in January 2009], it seems unlikely that the executive will be able to prevent a slew of habeas cases, which have, effectively, been held in a kind of legal gridlock for years, from progressing to court.

The only other obvious recourse, which will also help the prisoners to escape from the intolerable legal limbo in which they have been held for up to six and a half years, is that the administration will suddenly develop a previously undreamt-of diplomatic dexterity, and will make arrangements for the release of a large number of the 273 remaining prisoners without having to endure the acute embarrassment of justifying, in a proper courtroom, the hearsay, the innuendo, the generic information masquerading as evidence, and the fruits of torture, coercion and bribery that it has used to imprison these men for so many years.

Since 9/11 [the terrorist attacks of September 11, 2001], sadly, justice in the US has moved so slowly that on occasion it has appeared to be dead, but Thursday's verdict is a resounding triumph for the importance of the law as a check on unfettered executive power and the caprice of politicians. As Justice Kennedy stated in his opinion, "The laws and Constitution are designed to survive, and remain in force, in extraordinary times." He added, "To hold that the political branches may switch the Constitution on or off at will would lead to a regime in which they, not this court, say 'what the law is,'" a quote from an 1803 ruling, in which the Supreme Court explained its right to review acts of Congress, which, of course, reinforces the supremacy of the separation of powers that lies at the heart of the United States Constitution.

DNA and Legal Justice

Kevin Johnson

Kevin Johnson, a reporter for USA Today, *has written stories on terrorism, mentally incompetent defendants, and interrogation tactics by U.S. officials.*

In the following excerpt, reporter Kevin Johnson discusses the rapidly growing movement to release prisoners found to be innocent through DNA testing. Johnson writes that, since 1989, DNA testing has confirmed the innocence of 213 prisoners who had been incarcerated for crimes they did not commit. The state of Virginia alone is examining more than 534,000 files of convicted people to identify which cases warrant further scrutiny. Similar investigations have been launched in other states, including California, Arizona, and Texas.

After spending nearly 27 years buried in the vast Texas prison system for a crime he did not commit, Charles Chatman's first weeks of freedom have been overwhelming.

Each of the six rooms in his new apartment, including the bathroom, is larger than any of his previous cells. The gleaming entertainment system and sleek laptop from family, friends and attorneys might as well be hollow props on a movie set, because Chatman, 47, has little idea how to operate them— testimony to more than a generation lost behind bars.

Chatman was exonerated last month [January 2008] by DNA testing while serving a 99-year sentence for sexual assault. His release Jan. 3 marked the 15th such exoneration in Dallas County during the past five years, the most of any county in the nation. Aside from New York and Illinois, Dallas County also has produced more exonerations than any state.

Kevin Johnson, "DNA Tests Fuel Urgency to Free the Innocent," *USA TODAY*, February 18, 2008. Reproduced by permission.

Righting Injustices

As DNA technology and investigations identify a mounting number of wrongful convictions, the urgency to find others like Chatman is increasing. From Virginia to California, local prosecutors, law students and defense attorneys are combing through hundreds of thousands of old files in search of flawed convictions.

Last week, two men were cleared of separate murder convictions in Mississippi after new DNA testing led authorities to another man now charged in both slayings. It was the first time post-conviction DNA testing had led to an exoneration in Mississippi, one of eight states that does not have a law allowing for such testing. Lawyers with the Innocence Project [a national organization dedicated to exonerating wrongly convicted people] pushed the state to move forward with the testing.

Since 1989, there have been 213 post-conviction DNA exonerations in the USA. Of those, 149 came in the past seven years, according to the Innocence Project, the parent organization of a far-flung network that helps prisoners obtain DNA testing or other evidence that could prove their innocence.

Among efforts to ferret out the wrongfully convicted:

In Virginia, officials are conducting a sweeping examination of more than 534,000 files, the largest such review in U.S. history. Three years and five exonerations after the effort began, authorities have identified 2,215 more cases they say are worthy of scrutiny.

"If we identified (only) one guy who shouldn't be in prison, would it be worth it? I say yes," says Pete Marone, who as director of the state's Department of Forensic Science is helping to direct the review.

A team of attorneys and law students at California Western Law School, part of the national Innocence Project network, fields up to 1,000 inmate requests for help each year.

Jeff Chinn, assistant director of the Southern California Innocence Project, says 5% to 10% of those requests are selected for further investigation. Since the program began in 2000, five have been exonerated, including Timothy Atkins, who was freed last year [2007] after serving 20 years in prison for a wrongful murder conviction.

In Arizona, volunteer lawyers, law students and investigators have screened more than 2,500 cases in the past decade and secured one exoneration: Byron Lacy, freed in 2003 after serving six years for killing a security guard and wounding another man. About 20 other prisoners have won some kind of post-conviction relief, such as a shorter sentence.

In what may be the most aggressive move by a local prosecutor, Dallas County District Attorney Craig Watkins has turned over more than 400 files to law students working for the Innocence Project of Texas. The students are reviewing decisions by previous administrations to reject requests for DNA testing.

Watkins, Dallas County's first African-American district attorney, says opening the files may have been his easiest decision since being sworn in last year [2007], even in a state where politicians have a reputation for supporting aggressive law-and-order policies.

"The reason I'm here is a result of what happened in the past," Watkins says. He cites a tradition of aggressive prosecution in Dallas and routine denials of prisoners' requests for post-conviction reviews, which he says shrouded past errors. Those errors have emerged, Watkins says, largely because the local forensics laboratory preserved the biological evidence at issue in many of the recent challenges by prisoners.

For many places, a review of convictions such as that in Dallas County is not possible because physical evidence has not been preserved. The lack of uniform preservation standards is a big concern among advocates for post-conviction challenges, says Peter Neufeld, co-founder of the Innocence Project.

But for Watkins, the available evidence offered "an opportunity to restore the credibility of this office."

Judge Takes Interest in Case

In 17 years on the bench, Dallas Judge John Creuzot has heard countless defendants declare their innocence. But Chatman's 2001 application for post-conviction DNA testing was different.

"I noticed the guy had been inside for a long, long time," Creuzot says. At the time, Chatman had served 20 years of his 99-year sentence for rape.

It is rare for a prisoner to pursue a challenge after so long behind bars. Creuzot thought of boxer Rubin "Hurricane" Carter, freed after spending about 20 years in prison for the slayings of three men in New Jersey. Carter's case inspired the movie *Hurricane*.

"Maybe it was the movie," the judge says. "Something about (Chatman's case) caught me."

Chatman had lived in the same neighborhood as the rape victim. He was nearing the end of a four-year term of probation for a 1978 burglary conviction when she was attacked, and he was included in a police lineup of possible suspects. The victim identified him as her attacker, and he was convicted in 1981.

As Creuzot reviewed the file, the possible existence of untested DNA evidence and the identification of Chatman in the lineup—both among the most common reasons for a wrongful conviction—seemed to demand more scrutiny.

Months later, during Chatman's first appearance in Creuzot's courtroom, the judge says something else struck him, and raised questions about Chatman's guilt. "I can just remember his face when he said: 'I didn't do this. I didn't do this,'" he says.

A first attempt at DNA testing of the assailant's biological sample by the Texas Department of Public Safety did not produce a result, according to a chronology of the case prepared by the district attorney's office.

Chatman feared that further testing also would prove inconclusive and consume the biological sample—and with it, any chance of exoneration. Chatman and Michelle Moore, his attorney from the Innocence Project of Texas, asked that additional analysis be suspended in 2004 until testing technology improved.

Moore says Chatman showed remarkable judgment—and patience—in seeking the delay. "How many people would have done that?" she asks.

The opportunity for more reliable testing came last December [2007], when the judge ordered a new analysis using a method known as YSTR testing at Orchid Cellmark Inc., in nearby Farmers Branch, Texas. The new testing allows for better identification of male DNA profiles in samples in which female genetic material often is present, says Robert Giles, Orchid Cellmark's executive director of research and development.

Before ordering the test, Creuzot brought Chatman back to his office to see whether he wished to go forward, knowing that the new test—if inconclusive—likely would leave no more material to analyze.

"I asked him, 'Are you sure? This is it.'"

"Yes," Chatman responded. "I didn't do this."

At 8:30 a.m. on Jan. 2 [2008], weeks before results were due, the phone rang in Creuzot's office. Chatman's DNA was "not a match." Creuzot summoned an anxious Chatman from the county jail, where he was staying temporarily while awaiting the results.

"I knew what the test should say, but I still had that little doubt," Chatman says. "I had been a hard-luck guy for a long time."

When Chatman arrived, Creuzot stuck out his hand and said: "Man, Happy New Year!"

"He looked confused at first," the judge says. "I asked if he wanted to call somebody; I handed him my phone. He had never used a cellphone before, so I had to dial the number for him."

There was so much paperwork to process, Creuzot couldn't release Chatman immediately, so he ordered a celebratory lunch.

"I asked what kind of steak he wanted; he didn't know what to say, except to request that he wanted it 'cooked a lot,'" Creuzot says.

Chatman sat with the judge's 7-year-old son, Ethan, at a table in Creuzot's locked courtroom. (Ethan, on a holiday break from school, had accompanied his father to the office.) Chatman hadn't used a knife in years and began tearing the meat with his hands.

Lunch was one small measure of the seismic change in Chatman's world—a change Creuzot made official that day. He called the prison to inform the warden that Chatman was not coming back.

A "Logistical Nightmare"

Creuzot was instrumental in securing Chatman's release, but not all of the wrongfully convicted have found similar advocates.

Lack of funding for post-conviction analysis, including DNA testing and expert testimony, has hamstrung prisoner-assistance campaigns. The percentage of overturned cases is small, and the challenges are daunting.

Virginia's Marone calls the historic effort there to review thousands of old cases a "logistical nightmare."

The broad review, ordered more than two years ago by then-governor Mark Warner, was triggered in part by the discovery of blood and other potential biological evidence attached to old case files, some dating to 1973. The evidence had never been disclosed. The state began reviewing all of the files from 1973 to 1988, the time period at issue.

Because the files were not automated during that time, much of the project has required a hand-search of the documents in a labor-intensive and increasingly expensive examination. Marone says the analysis has cost about $1.4 million, and money is running out.

Virginia and the cash-strapped Arizona Justice Project had hoped to win some of the millions of dollars Congress set aside in 2006 to assist in DNA testing. Late last year [2007], *USA TODAY* disclosed that the Justice Department had not distributed any of the money.

"That is wrong," Senate Judiciary Chairman Patrick Leahy said last month [January 2008] at a hearing to address the issue. "That is irresponsible."

The Justice Department, which pledges to resolve the problem, had said that rules imposed by Congress made it difficult for states to qualify.

For example, the law requires that states' attorneys general compel police departments to preserve biological evidence for testing. However, attorneys general don't always have authority over the operations of all police agencies.

In Dallas County, much of the work to identify the wrongfully convicted is falling to law students and volunteer lawyers. Crowded into a small jury room in the Frank Crowley Courts Building, they leaf through thick case files, some more than three decades old.

Many of the students, drawn from local law schools, get no formal credit for the work. They work on all aspects of the cases, from re-interviewing witnesses to ensuring that those who are freed have new clothing when they leave prison.

Jessica Mines, 27, a second-year law student at Texas Wesleyan, says seeing the release of a prisoner like Chatman is "priceless."

Since Chatman's release, he has traveled to Washington, where he was welcomed at a Senate hearing and met briefly with Leahy, a vocal backer of legislation to help free the wrongfully convicted.

Chatman is eligible for up to $50,000 per year from the state for each of the 27 years of lost time. He is weighing a lawsuit over his incarceration and will get the state money only if he decides not to sue.

His family and attorneys provide much of what he has—the apartment, furniture and a new pickup. He earned a general educational development (GED) certificate in prison and is considering enrolling in college, or pursuing a career as a welder or auto mechanic.

For now, the new truck mostly sits in a parking space because he fears he'll lose his way if he strays too far from his sprawling apartment complex. But there are plenty of other options for life outside his cell.

"I can just go take a bath," he says, "and lay in the tub any time I want."

For Further Discussion

1. How do you think Arthur Miller's life and early work led to and prepared him for writing *The Crucible*? (See Helterman, Hogan, and Centola.)

2. In what ways does Miller see parallels between the Salem witch trials and McCarthyism? (See Arthur Miller.)

3. How does fanatical religion contribute to injustice? (See Adler, Fender, Welland, and Timothy Miller.)

4. Discuss the specific legal rights that are denied the accused in Salem and the detainees at U.S. Naval Base Guantanamo Bay. (See Porter, Bigsby, Martine, Brasch, and Worthington.)

5. How do the government and the individuals' consciences clash in *The Crucible*? (See Arthur Miller, Timothy Miller, Griffin, and Bhatia).

6. Discuss the issue of evidence in *The Crucible*. (See Arthur Miller, and Fender.)

For Further Reading

Arthur Miller, *After the Fall*. New York: Viking, 1964.

———, *All My Sons*. New York: Reynal and Hitchcock, 1947.

———, *Death of a Salesman*. New York: Viking, 1949.

———, *Incident at Vichy*. New York: Viking, 1965.

———, *The Price*. New York: Viking, 1968.

———, *Timebends*. New York: Grove, 1987.

———, *A View from the Bridge*. London: Cresset, 1957.

Bibliography

Books

Herbert Blau "The Whole Man and the Real Witch." In *Arthur Miller: A Collection of Critical Essays*. Ed. Robert W. Corrigan. Englewood Cliffs, NJ: Prentice-Hall, 1969.

Steven Brill *After: Rebuilding and Defending America in the September 12 Era.* New York: Simon and Schuster, 2003.

Neil Carson *Arthur Miller.* New York: Grove Press, 1982.

Joan DelFattore "Fueling the Fire of Hell: A Reply to Censors of *The Crucible*." In *Censored Books: Critical Viewpoints*. Ed. Nicholas Karolides, et al. Metuchen, NJ: Scarecrow Press, 1993.

John H. Ferres *Twentieth-Century Interpretations of "The Crucible."* Englewood Cliffs, NJ: Prentice-Hall, 1972.

Morris Freedman *American Dream in Social Context.* Carbondale: Southern Illinois University Press, 1971.

Ronald Hayman *Arthur Miller.* New York: Frederick Ungar, 1972.

Edmund S. Morgan	"Arthur Miller's *The Crucible* and the Salem Witch Trials: A Historian's View." In *The Golden and Brazen World: Papers in Literature and History 1650–1800.* Ed. John M. Wallace. Berkeley: University of California Press, 1985.
Leonard Moss	*Arthur Miller.* New York: Twayne, 1967.
Edward Murray	*Arthur Miller.* New York: Ungar, 1971.
Benjamin Nelson	*Arthur Miller: Portrait of a Playwright.* London: Peter Owen, 1970.
Sidney H. White	*Guide to Arthur Miller.* Columbus, OH: Merrill, 1970.
Nada Zeineddine	*Because It Is My Name.* Devon, UK: Merlin, 1991.

Periodicals

Jennifer Allen	"Miller's Tale," *New York*, vol. 16, January 24, 1983.
David Bergeron	"Arthur Miller's *The Crucible* and Nathaniel Hawthorne: Some Parallels," *English Journal*, vol. 58, 1969.
Jean-Marie Bonnet	"Society vs. the Individual in Arthur Miller's *The Crucible*," *English Studies*, vol. 63, February 1982.

Matthew Hay Brown   "At Camp Iquana, the Enemies Are Children," *Hartford Courant*, July 20, 2003.

Tom Brune   "Rights Abuses Probed," *Newsday*, July 22, 2003.

John Ditsky   "Stone, Fire, and Light: Approaches to *The Crucible*," *North Dakota Quarterly*, vol. 46, no. 2, 1978.

Gary P. Hendrickson   "The Last Analogy. Arthur Miller's Witches and America's Domestic Communists," *Midwest Quarterly*, vol. 33, no. 4, 1992.

Freda Kirchwey   "The Crucible," *Nation*, vol. 176, February 7, 1953.

Stephen Marino   "Arthur Miller's 'Weight of Truth,'" *Modern Drama*, vol. 38, Winter 1995.

Robert A. Martin   "Arthur Miller: Public Issues, Private Tensions," *Studies in the Literary Imagination*, vol. 21, no. 2, 1988.

William McGill Jr.   "The Crucible of History: Arthur Miller's John Proctor," *New England Quarterly*, vol. 54, June 1981.

Henry Popkin   "Arthur Miller's *The Crucible*," *College English*, vol. 26, November 1964.

Red Channels   "Arthur Miller," June 1950.

Judd Slivka   "Terrorists Planned to Set Wild Fires, FBI Warned," *Arizona Republic*, July 12, 2003.

Philip Walker   "Arthur Miller's *The Crucible*:
                     Tragedy or Allegory?" *Western Speech*,
                     vol. 20, 1956.

Robert Warshow   "The Liberal Conscience in *The
                     Crucible*," *Commentary*, vol. 15,
                     March 1953.

Index